The Ultimate
DECORATING
Book

The Ultimate DECORATING Book

Over 1,000 decorating ideas for all the rooms in your home

COLLINS & BROWN

First published in 1998 by Kiln House Books
Kiln House, 210 New Kings Road
London SW6 4NZ

This edition published by Collins & Brown Limited 1999
London House, Great Eastern Wharf
Parkgate Road, London SW11 4NQ

1 3 5 7 9 8 6 4 2

ISBN 1-85585-753-7

Editor: Claire Waite
Writers: Ann Boston and Jane Hughes
Art Editor: Chris Wood
Designers: Alison Shackleton and Ruth Prentice

Reproduction by Colour Symphony, Singapore
Printed and bound by Toppan, China

Contents

INTRODUCTION 6

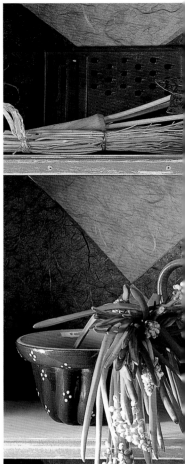

Introduction

Home decorating becomes an exciting prospect if you think of yourself as the artist and your home as a blank canvas ready and waiting. The colors, the styles, and the materials you use to create the look and atmosphere you want are your own choice, your own unique palette. What might at first seem a daunting task can become a creative challenge, and an opportunity to learn all sorts of skills of the trade.

INTRODUCTION

The very first decorating thought which usually comes to mind is about what colors to use in a scheme – what we like, what will look good, what shades and combinations work well together. Considerations of color are also fascinating and fun, with all those little paint samples from suppliers to collect and strong opinions from all the occupants of the home. But before you go too far along the color path, some other basic decorating considerations need to be addressed.

Alongside color, you also need to consider the functions that the room you are about to decorate must fulfill: the amount and quality of natural light; the atmosphere you wish to create; and your budget. It is no good dreaming up a sumptuous boudoir of velvets and gold leaf and antique mahogany if you need a workaday family room achieved at very little cost. Neither would it be advisable to indulge your taste for midnight blue in a small, north-facing room with only one tiny window.

So that the gap between inspiration and reality does not become too depressing, you could start with two lists, one of your ideals and decorating desires, and the other with practicalities and what you can afford, then try to fit them together to form a whole plan. For example, you may want the clean lines and crisp whites of a minimal decorating scheme, but the room is to be played in by your children, along with their sticky fingers. You might then think about designing ingenious storage so that toys can be swept away to leave the space uncluttered, and consider a high tech gray color, instead of white, which will still look cool and calm while disguising greasy marks.

Next, you need to stand back and look at the blank canvases of your existing rooms. If you are moving into a new and undecorated house this is easy, but if you are redecorating it is more difficult to blank out what is already there. Try to visualize the room empty of furniture and fixtures and half-close your eyes to blur any existing patterns and colors. Think of the room almost in abstract terms, as a series of linked surfaces – the walls, the ceiling, and the floor – and look at the shapes they make together and the amount of light reflected off them. This will give you some basic ideas about the styles and colors which might be suitable

Now you can begin to think about color and style. Light and bright colors will give life and interest to small rooms, while dark colors will make large, cold rooms more intimate and inviting. The size, proportions, shapes, and architectural features of the room might suggest a particular style, as might a view from the windows or the functions the room will have to accommodate. A family bathroom with a round porthole window, for example, is an obvious candidate for a ship's interior treatment; a dining room with French doors opening onto the garden might suggest airy greens and yellows and a country treatment of simple checks and ginghams.

Then you need to do lots of looking – at other rooms in other houses to see what you like and what you don't think works, and at books and magazines to pick out color

RIGHT: This is where you could be when the decorating is over: treating friends to an elegant lunch in the dappled light of the sun-room! Warm whites, natural wood, brick, and metal allow the trees and the blue sky to take center stage.

schemes and decorating styles which are attractive and might achieve your ends. It is worth collecting a little file of tear-sheets from magazines and of photographs of rooms which you like, together with paint samples and swatches of fabrics and flooring materials available from manufacturers. It is very difficult to make a quick decision about decorating and well worth looking around, collecting bits and pieces, and pondering for a few weeks or months. Neither do you have to do it all in one go. Once a room is painted or papered and the skeleton furnishings in place, you can live in it for a while before deciding on the right lampshade or the arrangement of pictures on a wall.

However you manage it, there must be a starting point for your design and color considerations. Once the basics are firmly in mind it could be something as simple as a treasured rug or a collection of colorful pottery that gets your scheme underway. The natural dyes and abstract patterns of a kilim might suggest an

BELOW: The white and gold shades of polished soft wood, woven rushes, and a watery paint used on the walls, are the only colors needed to decorate this seashore bathroom.

oriental flavor, with spice colors; the brilliant blues of glazed earthenware to be displayed on a wall might look fantastic against a strong yellow paint. Hints such as these could be enough to get your ideas up and running. Your inspiration does not have to be complicated or dramatic to succeed.

Your imagination need not be limited by the area where you live. You can have a country-style room in the middle of the city, or create an urban loft space in a rural barn. As long as you keep a measured eye on the scale and proportions of the spaces and on the architectural integrity of the building, you can move on to achieve the look or atmosphere of your dreams without inhibition. A green and natural look might be just what you want to escape into after a busy day of city life. You can also enhance your home's good points and disguise those which are not so attractive, making the best of its limitations and drawing attention to its best architectural features.

BELOW: An inexpensive hardwood table, frottaged in a rich terra-cotta, decorated with stenciled patterns, and heavily varnished, looks as though it has been in the dining room for centuries.

Once you have your whole scheme – its colors, materials, furnishings, and details – decided and set in stone, wait a few days, then go back and try to loosen it up a little. If everything matches perfectly and is chosen and positioned as though in a museum, the room will look contrived and unwelcoming. Throw one extra color into the palette you have already chosen, or use cushion fabrics which don't have the same textures as the curtains, as originally planned, and it will all shake down to a scheme which then seems much more natural, one thrown together with effortless good taste and individuality.

Whatever you do, make a bold statement if you want to, and don't let someone who is a nervous commentator persuade you to water down your ideas. If you have based your plan on cobalt blue walls, the end result will be tepid and disappointing if you balk at the paint store counter and buy cans of a safe sky blue instead. Go for it; don't be scared. Equally, don't be tempted to include anything just because it is fashionable or perceived by others to be in good taste. Your efforts will only work if they represent what you like; it is impossible to

RIGHT: The painted decoration of this room couldn't be more simple, the interest and impact of the scheme being made by a table draped with two colorful, Provençal printed tablecloths.

BELOW: A wonderful feeling of warmth and relaxation is created here by a clever combination of rich reds, greens, and yellows, with hints of gold. The vase of haphazard spring flowers pulls all the colors together.

choose a room style and get it right when you don't like the elements you are putting into it. And, even when the whole prospect of decorating becomes almost too much to contemplate, try not to lose a lightness of touch: a decorative scheme which takes itself too seriously can seem dead. It actively lifts the spirits to live with a little fun and fantasy.

To get you started as a confident and cheerful home decorator, there is a whole mass of different styles, inspirational ideas, techniques, and practical tips in the pages which follow. From deciding upon a decorative scheme, through the nitty-gritty of painting and decorating and working with soft furnishings, to the finishing touches of arranging pictures and flowers, this is the ultimate guide to decorating success and satisfaction. Good luck and good decorating!

ABOVE: It's all in the soft furnishings: three rather daring and unusual colors are combined to create the effect and character in this living room, highlighted by the matching vases of tulips.

OPPOSITE: An otherwise boring chest of small drawers becomes great fun, with each drawer painted a different color at random. Brightly colored plant pots and kitchen utensils continue the theme.

DECORATING WITH STYLE

Introduction

The way you live, spend your time, and decorate your living space is a matter of personal choice. Finding a style that suits you, and taking your courage in both hands to follow it through, is the first crucial step to decorating success.

LEFT: *Bold floral chair covers cheerfully combine with fresh lilac and peppermint, without obsessively repeating the color scheme.*

RIGHT: *Even the most workmanlike corner can be given charm by harmonious use of color and accessories.*

ABOVE: Learning to work within the framework of a strong but simple color scheme can be an exhilarating and rewarding experience.

ABOVE RIGHT: A kitchen collection of china in predominant shades of green and yellow, displayed on open shelving, could define both style and color choice in a kitchen.

Traditional country? Contemporary geometric? Cool neutrals? Whatever your own decorating preference, other factors must be taken into account. The age and design of the building itself; the size and layout of the rooms; your practical living requirements; and any furniture and accessories you already have, all need to be considered. If you are starting out with a blank slate, so much the better! An empty room can be the ultimate decorator's luxury. The trick is to recognize the basic elements of a style and experiment with them. Start with color, then go on to floor treatments, textiles, and lighting. Or sometimes flooring can dictate the decor of a room or hallway: use it to define your choice. You could begin with something treasured, however small: designers have planned whole rooms around a single textile, a collection of jugs, or even a favorite armchair.

LEFT: *This strong orange-on-white colorwash contrasted with dark blue-gray woodwork looks dramatic in daylight and warm at night, showing how effective color and paint effects can be.*

OPPOSITE: *The classic elegance of pure linen comes within reach of the tightest budget, in a panel blind made of linen tea towels for a kitchen window.*

ABOVE: *A thrift-shop cupboard gets the treatment. Stripped, polished, painted inside, and with a traditional lace trim, it becomes the perfect frame for country ceramics whose painted flowers are echoed by pots of dried roses.*

Grand ideas and bold plans thrive on thrift. The spare perfection of Scandinavian style, epitomized by the artist Carl Larsson, relied far more on creativity than on cost.

Look afresh at your room, free of furniture if possible. Are you using it to its full potential? Could you make a dark corner more enticing with mirrors or new lighting, or release living-room space by turning over an unused hall area to storage? A fresh coat of paint using new colors is the most obvious and simple way to transform a room. Stretch a tight budget to maximum effect by recycling old pieces of furniture; stripped or repainted and stenciled, they can enhance your new look. Junk-shop finds can look rich and rare transformed by new coverings or a lick of paint. Fresh slipcovers, or a scatter of cushions and a bright new throw, can transform a dingy living room or bedroom.

Choosing Colors

Choosing your paint colors is probably the hardest decorating decision you will make. Don't be daunted: allow time to experiment. Consider your colors as you would a love affair. Much as you enjoy their company, would you want to live with them?

LEFT: *Bright yellow walls, natural rattan and wicker, and green leaves create a sunny, mellow interior climate.*

RIGHT: *Part of the fun of decorating is in mixing a palette of unexpected shades that work together.*

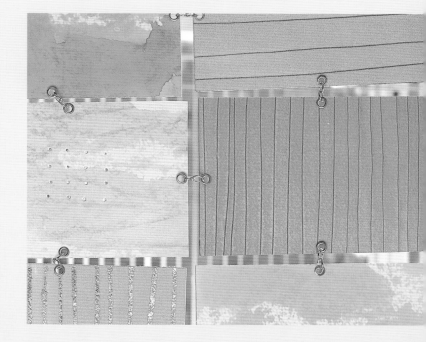

ABOVE: Anemones vibrantly show the color range from red through pink to purple.

Color Confidence

Given that choosing colors is so much a question of personal taste, why not start with the ones that attract you most? Remember, though, that color is not static. The same shade can look quite different in daylight or under artificial light, in matte or gloss finish, or used on a cupboard or on walls. Also, a color becomes hugely intensified over a large area.

Imagining the order of the colors in a rainbow spectrum can help with combining colors. The three primaries – red, blue, and yellow – are intersected by the secondaries – violet, orange, and green – each color shading into its neighbor. Between them are tertiaries: turquoise, mixing blue and green, for instance. Warm colors – yellow, orange, red – are known as "advancing" colors, while cool blues, grays, dark greens, purple are "retreating." Some colors, known as "complementary" colors, produce a neutral shade and balance each other when mixed equally together.

LEFT: *In this still life of purples and greens, the naturally harmonious contrasts in the ripening plums find echoes in the blue-green dish and rich purple throw edged with plum-colored velvet.*

OPPOSITE: *These accessories in royal blue, yellow, and green balance the deep red wall and fruit, reducing their dominance.*

Brights

Brilliant, sizzling color – cheerful, extrovert, exuberant – gives a real boost to the spirits. Think of a field of red poppies, or golden sunflowers turning to face the sun. Many people find a dash of bright color in details like cushions, flowers, or ceramics is enough to lift the quieter base colors they choose for their surroundings. More confident temperaments use hot, attention-seeking reds and yellows as their main theme. The more intense a color, the greater its purity, and the less gray it contains. Remember that flat, opaque color can be inert and hard; broken by texture and pattern, however, it becomes atmospheric and alive.

ABOVE RIGHT: The luminous depth of colorwashed burnt ocher walls harmonizes with heavy, gold velvet drapes, while the vivid yellow flowers by the window draw sunshine into the room.

RIGHT: Scarlet is dominant in this dazzling display. The tendency of red to overpower the eye is broken by complementary blues in the richly textured embroidered cushion, stained glass, and blue-gray foliage.

RIGHT: *Flashes of high-voltage color look stunning displayed against natural wood or brilliant white. Or pick your background color from one of the paints used to decorate the dish.*

BELOW: *A glowing centerpiece of flowerheads in the flame-color spectrum of yellows, oranges, and reds offers a radiant welcome to guests. Bright floating candles add luminous intensity to the theme.*

Pastels

Lighter shades of a color brighten dark rooms and are softer on the eye than fully saturated color. The paler tints of pink, violet, pale blues, and greens are gentle and restful to live with; they are generally seen as "feminine" colors and are often used in bedrooms, teamed with lace or voile curtains and muslin drapes. Brighter sherbet shades work especially well together, combining different hues of similar strength, and are popular with modern designers who use them in solid, matte finishes for a fresh, clean look. Delicate washes of pastel shades, especially pearly gray, blue, and cream, are a hallmark of Swedish style. A thin, cool color can be enriched by a layer of glaze or watercolor in a softer, deeper shade, which lends itself to a country-style setting.

ABOVE: Dried flower colors of lavender and mauve, often partnered by soft mint green and apricot, look equally good used in a traditional country or a contemporary setting.

RIGHT: The cool, dreamy mood set by pale, violet-gray walls is cleverly accentuated in the mirror with its framing pattern of clouds or waves. The gray-green leaves, translucent glass vase, and antique gold details contribute to the restful atmosphere.

RIGHT: Bright pastels on a cream ground add a fresh, light feel to the bedroom. The quilt's contemporary design emphasizes the colors through intriguing shapes and stitchings. Pastel sheets repeat the bedcover's color theme.

RIGHT: Pastels equal pure nostalgia in this traditional teatime scene in shades of pale pink and green, with a dash of pale yellow.

Earthy Tones

Ocher, sienna, umber, terra-cotta, the brownish reds are the earth colors. The first colors used by man, the natural pigments are clays, although today most pigment is chemically made. These handsome rusty, spicy hues look superb in Italian frescoes and house exteriors under hot sun. Transferred to the walls of a contemporary building, they can look muddy, unless used with the right furniture and finishes. They are superb teamed with olive or dusty blue-gray woodwork; a splash of peacock blue can look stunning against an umber ground. Earthy colors respond especially well to rough surfaces and distressing and colorwash treatments, which break their flatness and bring them to life. A sophisticated contemporary look contrasts rough, rustic plaster walls with highly polished aluminum or chrome fixtures and furniture.

ABOVE: Rusts are warm, comfortable, kitchen or garden-room classics: terra-cotta floor tiles with scrubbed or polished wood, for example.

LEFT: *Earthy hues are classic country colors, especially compatible with olive and bottle green. Note the contrast between matte burnt-sienna walls and the shiny patina on the paler ceiling.*

RIGHT: *Restful shades of cream, buttermilk, and white with stripped timber flooring are teamed here with quiet green, the colors of foliage, and natural materials. A decorative border adds unfussy interest to a plain roller shade.*

ABOVE: *The classic purity of form and the "natural" crackle pattern of the glaze in a Japanese bowl show how the attention focuses on fine detail when sensation-seeking.*

LEFT: *The nubbly texture and cool feel of antique linen is a key component of a neutral, natural color scheme, along with unbleached cottons, burlap (hessian), and slubbed silks. Look for or add borders, seams, and embroidery to provide textural interest.*

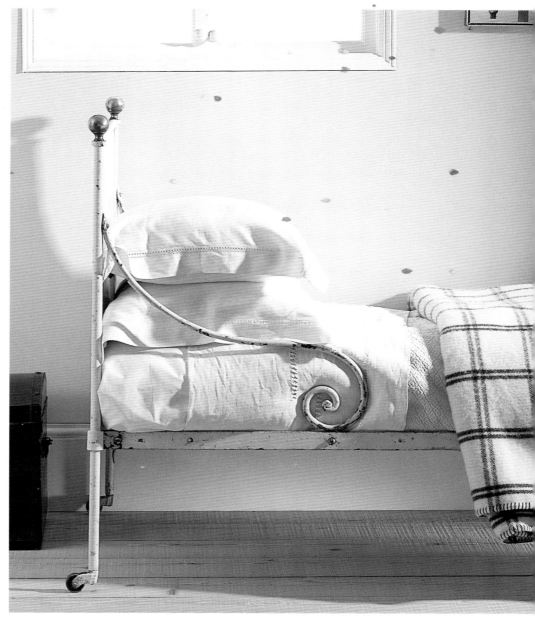

ABOVE: *The simple lines of a painted wrought-iron bedstead, the fresh linen, bedcover, and the walls are all white or off-white, yet texture and form provide plenty of interest. The blue-checked blanket adds a touch of color without being overwhelming.*

Understated Shades

When color is removed from a room, the eye is drawn instead to texture and shape. Light becomes especially important, since it highlights surfaces and shadows. Think of shades of oatmeal, sand, stone, ivory, cream, biscuit, oyster; of pale timber floors, driftwood, unbleached fabrics, and white china – all ingredients of this restrained, modern look. Architects love the discreet charm of neutrals and naturals, whose lightness and warmth enhance a display of well-chosen furniture or an art collection.

ABOVE: *Blue and white is a favorite color combination in many different cultures and contexts. Its fresh, clean look is a favorite for bathrooms and kitchens, as here, where blue-and-white china on the hutch (dresser) counterpoints blue detailing in the dining room.*

Blues

Blue, the color of the sky and sea, is strongly associated with peace and harmony, and loved the world over for its calming influence. The range of shades is enormous, from the palest baby blue to deepest midnight. In between there are cool Scandinavian powder and pearly blues; fresh duck-egg and turquoise; faded denim; the smoky blue that was favored by the Shakers; clear bright azure, seen on shutters and doors all around the

RIGHT: The vogue for blue-and-white ceramics began in China centuries ago, spreading through Islamic countries to Italy, Holland, and English Worcester, willow pattern, and Wedgwood china. Contemporary versions are spatterware and "flow blue."

BELOW: Clear Mediterranean blue gives fresh life to old furniture like this chair, or to kitchen shelves.

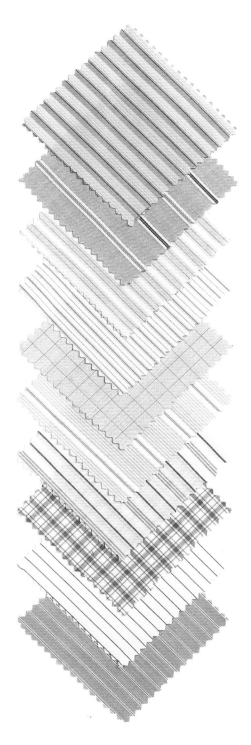

Mediterranean; pure lapis lazuli and deep, rich indigo; and dark Prussian, navy, and royal blue.

Blue is highly dependent on light: for instance, the magnificent deep blues used in Moorish design under strong sunshine can look strident in thin northern daylight. It also varies with the colors put with it, becoming warmer with red, cooler with green. Blue and yellow, both primary colors, are an especially happy combination of contrasting hues, in which yellow adds warmth and vitality to blue's coolness.

ABOVE: Blue-and-white stripes and checks have a perennial appeal, and combine well with each other or with other patterns. Note the affinity with sand and other earth colors.

Reds

The strongest color in the spectrum, red, is the color of fire and warning, and is children's top favorite for its in-your-face, traffic-stopping appeal. Used in decorating, red has great dramatic impact. It can also be unexpectedly romantic as it shades away from color-saturated crimson, scarlet, and poppy: think of deep red roses and romantic pinks, of warm orange- and brown-tinged coral, brick and russet, and the dark jewel-like shades of ruby, mulberry, and wine. Exotic, spicy Indian reds, terra-cotta, and pinkish fuchsia and magenta are easier to incorporate into a color scheme, being less dominant than the primary reds, although these can be used to spectacular effect with the right combination of partner colors. The Victorian British popularized the red dining room as a rich, intimate atmosphere for entertaining. A single wall painted in the glowing, polished red of Chinese lacquerwork adds vibrancy to a geometric interior. Gilt accessories look especially rich against a red wall.

ABOVE: The warm brick red, broken by rough brush strokes, in these handpainted dishes teams well with distressed green and cream woodwork. A little red can go a long way; here the effect is bright and cheerful, without becoming overpowering.

RIGHT: Soft cherry reds marry well with blue-gray, gray-green, and creamy yellow – a pretty combination with 1930s period appeal.

OPPOSITE: Bold swathes of clear mandarin red are used to stunning effect with apple green, white, and touches of apricot. An example of how a potentially dominant "advancing" color can be knocked back by clever, unexpected coordination with a complementary hue.

Yellows

One of the most popular colors on the decorator's palette, yellow is also the most difficult to get right. Given its affinity with the sun and summer, it is surprising how cold or muddy a tint can become over a large area, so it is well worth trying out paints and textiles before leaping to a decision. Remember too that yellow is very responsive to lighting and paint effects; it likes texture and usually looks better applied to walls than furniture. One of the three primary colors, its spectrum includes acid yellow; bright buttercup and sunflower; earthy ocher, mustard, turmeric, saffron; gold; and orangey apricots.

Creamy yellow walls with dusty blue paintwork is a traditional combination in the Shaker look. English country house style favors warm buttery yellows for the kitchen, hallway, or living room, while a sophisticated contemporary look partners pale primrose with gray. The muddier ochers are a marvelous foil for cobalt blue or Indian red.

ABOVE: Yellow responds to colors put with it, and has an affinity with green.

ABOVE: The fresh yellow of lemons matches their sharp, acidic taste. Lemon walls suit an elegant Empire-style drawing room; lemon silk is handsome with deep blue, or gray and white; other sherbet shades give it a modern look.

LEFT: *Primary yellow is a bright and cheerful choice for a breakfast room, applied as broken color on the walls for a lively and less intense finish. The yellow and green theme for the stenciled chairs and table is repeated in the colorwashed paneling.*

43

Greens

The wonderful variety of greens in foliage has given us the names for many different shades: sage, moss, grass, fern, apple, mint . . . Its associations with nature, with forests and gardens, make it a quiet, contemplative color, easy to live with and combine with others. Green is a secondary color, made by mixing blue and yellow, and its character depends on which of the two is stronger. A popular contemporary kitchen color is a mid-blue-green which blends the two colors in equal strengths.

Deep greens have strong masculine connotations, emphasized by names such as racing, hunting, and bottle green; these and forest or Brunswick green are traditionally used for front doors and wooden clapboard exteriors, and inside for studies and halls. Teamed with tartans and Regency stripes, they create a comfortable, clubby atmosphere.

Mid-greens are predominant in chintzes, evocative of summer country gardens. Soft gray-green and pale mint green are much-loved ingredients in country house style. Acid green is a favorite contemporary color, and is combined with orange, metallic blue, or mauve for a sharp, modern look.

ABOVE: *Natural inspiration, in the bluish bloom on greengage plums, shows green's affinity with gold and verdigris, highly effective on antiqued furniture.*

RIGHT: *Deep, rich green tapestries, silk taffetas, and heavy velvets add formal luxury to a dining room, book-lined office or study, or living room.*

OPPOSITE: *Soft willow-green and cream, ideally suited to country style, bring the garden into the house.*

LEFT: *This symphony in green is proof of the color's friendly versatility. Touches of pure saturated emerald counter the sage curtains and apple-green chair, while the bold, checked wallpaper, which could be dominant in another color, successfully harmonizes in green.*

Contrasting Colors

Getting bright colors to "sing" together demands strong nerves and patient experimenting. The results can be hugely rewarding, bringing a charge of energy to your living space. Great artists like Matisse and Bonnard were masters of color, and their work is full of inspiration. Successful combinations often juxtapose colors of equal brightness or tone. The competing colors of flowers in a garden are a good place to start: brilliant vermilion and magenta geraniums with bright green leaves, sapphire blue delphiniums and orange marigolds all hold their own and balance each other.

Red and green are complementary colors, at far ends of the spectrum, and work especially strongly together. Remember too that dark colors retreat and light ones advance when you look at them: a shocking pink cushion on a royal blue sofa draws your attention to the pink, and makes the sofa appear to recede.

LEFT: *Imagination rather than expense is the secret to combining strong colors and flowing materials to tremendously stylish effect. The glowing folds of these rich blue chenille curtains, galvanized by their acid-yellow scooped valance drape, give stunning focus to a window.*

LEFT: *Nature is extravagant with color – why shouldn't we be? A chorus line of poster-color flowers with their bright green leaves, planted in cheerful painted yellow and red pots, has maximum impact against a backdrop of cool fondant blue that contains a touch of red.*

LEFT: *Purple, violet, and magenta are among the most vibrant colors in the spectrum. Each is a composite of red and blue, so mixing them with dissonant reds and blues is a form of color marriage. Jewel-bright hues are favorites of traditional folk art decoration.*

BELOW: *These eggs have been painted in soft glowing colors which are buffed back and overlaid with a broken gilded finish. A marbled mantelpiece or accessories with a tinge of color breaking through can subtly enhance the shade you have chosen for walls or paintwork.*

RIGHT: *Raw silk, linen, and burlap (hessian) have a golden sheen which teams beautifully with cream, white, or broken dusty pink. Shades of terra-cotta, pink, straw, white, mint, and lilac have all been successfully incorporated in the idiosyncratic curtain tieback.*

Toning Muted Shades

The muted pinks and grays of a woodpigeon's feathers, iridescent mother-of-pearl, or the faded colors of dried flowers, are among the subtlest and most beautiful in the natural palette. The effect depends on minute gradations of one tone of a color to the next (lighter or darker), or from one color to its neighbor in the color spectrum. The natural sheen on silks and linens, feathers, shells, eggs, and semi-precious stones is an essential element in this light, airy, feminine look. Shades of gold, cream, and white are among its leading lights; dusty pink, lilac, mint are other components. Broken texture, in the form of distressed paint effects with antiqued gold or verdigris finishes, or colorwashed walls, softens the effect of flat color; glazes and satin paint finishes add patina.

ABOVE: Cream and gold allow the delicate textures of fine lace and latticed creamware ceramics to reveal themselves in a light, feminine style evocative of times past. Cream paints add warmth and depth to a country kitchen or bedroom, and look lovely with faded chintz.

Country Style

The comfortable appeal of country style is timeless and versatile. Warm and evocative, its benchmarks of simplicity, natural materials, and functional design have made it equally suited to traditional or contemporary tastes, and easily adaptable for town or country living.

LEFT: *The ingredients of country style: scrubbed and waxed pine furniture, tiled or flagged floors, earthenware crocks and blue-and-white dishes.*

RIGHT: *The style evokes the myth – of home cooking and fresh garden produce.*

Rural Nostalgia

Nostalgia for rural life seems to become stronger as our lives are drawn away from the country and into the city. Ever more frenetic, often insecure lifestyles make us long for stability, enduring priorities, and the comforting authority of tradition.

Rustic style, embodied in the rocking chair beside the hearth and its hospitable comforts, symbolizes our continuing need for family values and homestead conventions. It recalls the self-sufficient virtues of thrift and good housekeeping betokened by a pretty quilt pieced from worn-out clothes, logs waiting by the wood-burning stove, and a pantry stocked with produce from the kitchen garden. Rough-hewn stone and plaster, seasoned timber beams, soft pastel limewashes, folk-art decorations, and ready hospitality dispensed from the kitchen table are all part of the look. If the way of life that evolved it has largely vanished, the simplicity of this style makes it perennially and widely adaptable.

LEFT: *The rough-and-ready stone hearth offers warmth and welcome, emphasized by dried flowers, a gentle stenciled design on the wall surround, and a fresh lace mantelshelf trim.*

ABOVE: *Garden herbs hung up to dry are a decorative display of household provender.*

LEFT: *Farmhouse baking, natural materials, and strong textures are the order of the day.*

The Country Kitchen

Traditionally the heart of the home, the kitchen continues to be the informal center of the household, where family members meet and talk across the table at mealtimes. In the past people naturally congregated in the warmest room of the house, heated by the cooking range which was constantly stoked for boiling kettles and keeping ovens hot. In recent decades, architects' attempts to banish messy food preparation to a small back room have been continually foiled by homemakers who knock down partitions and open up living space so that the cook shares the "sociable kitchen" with family and friends.

Today the refinements of the modern country kitchen have banished the worst elements of the original version – smoke and dust from solid-fuel stoves, small windows, poor ventilation – while keeping the best of its intrinsic style. The twentieth-century kitchen range, the Aga, still performs the same role of general comforter and cook's best friend.

Tradition continues through painted wooden paneling, glass-fronted cupboards that display dishes, and sturdy worktables used for both preparing and eating food. The fitted kitchen, status symbol of the fifties and sixties, is sometimes giving way again to freestanding country furniture – the hutch (dresser) and the sideboard. In an age which sees cooking as an enjoyable hobby, the country kitchen is as much in demand as ever.

ABOVE: *The country look is strengthened by distressed walls, solid pine furniture, and accessories like wicker baskets and hampers.*

RIGHT: *Every home should have one: the spice rack displaying its ranks of storage jars is a country style essential.*

OPPOSITE: *Fragrant dried flowers hanging from the drying rack add a traditional touch to the user-friendly, contemporary country kitchen.*

ABOVE: *A perfect example of form following function, the hutch (dresser) was designed for use as both serving table and storage. The dishes are displayed on shelves rather than hidden in cupboards, making a blue-and-white dinner service or a collection of china into a decorative feature.*

RIGHT: *Fresh, unsophisticated floral fabrics create an inviting yet informal atmosphere in the country kitchen. Pink and cream paintwork with a hint of green, echoed in the green dishes, is a pretty, traditional color scheme easily compatible with contemporary living.*

BELOW: Kitchen chairs and tables acquire a fresh new look with a coat of paint, here matching the pretty hand-stenciled curtain fabric.

An important feature of the country kitchen is the dining area, the household's meeting and eating place. This should be both functional and inviting, incorporating storage for crockery and utensils as well as space for sitting comfortably around the table. Chairs are plain or painted wood, rather than elaborately upholstered, and floors need to be easily cleaned of crumbs and debris: stone flags, ceramic tiles, and varnished or stained boards are popular options. Displays of fruit, vegetables, and flowers are colorful and welcoming.

RIGHT: *Instant country look in a bedroom under the eaves is created by a stenciled floral design and leafy border on the walls, a fresh alternative to wallpaper, along with flower-embroidered bedcover and pillows.*

Wildflowers

Part of the appeal of country style lies in the unselfconscious charm of its floral patterns, so evocative of delicate wildflowers. A posy of meadow flowers has a beauty unmatched by any exotic florist's display. Cornflowers, poppies, primroses, forget-me-nots, and many more are lovingly reproduced on chintz, embroidered textiles, stenciled paint effects, china, enamelware, and so on. Floral textiles in particular have been popular for centuries: sprigged muslins were all the rage in Jane Austen's day, and the phenomenal success of Liberty prints and Laura Ashley fabrics in recent years owed much to their distinctive

LEFT: A plain wooden bedstead acquires country style with a coat of blue paint stenciled with a red-and-gold flower motif. The same stencil has been used on the plain cotton bedcover to echo the floral theme.

floral designs. Wildflowers were also a distinctive feature of Arts and Crafts textiles, inspired by medieval tapestries and still popular today; printed on a deep, rich colorbase, their delicate shapes acquire strength and intensity.

Different flower prints or designs can be used together if you follow certain basic rules. One secret of success is to combine different patterns of the same size and colorway, otherwise the larger one will overwhelm the smaller. It is also safest to use fabrics of similar weight and texture: modest cottons and rich silks can sit uncomfortably together, or instance. A pretty, contemporary country look is to line floral print curtains with matching checks or stripes.

Checks and Tartans

Checks, in their many forms, are a brilliantly versatile way of using patterns. You can find them in every color and size, from the smallest pindot to great window-pane squares, and they cheerfully mix and match with other designs.

LEFT: *Simple blue-and-white checks add a fresh look to a hallway. Full-length checked curtains could be too much but the integral valance and blind are lively and bright.*

RIGHT: *The geometric lines of checks and tartans hold the boldest colors together.*

Gingham

Where would we be without gingham? The name comes from the Malay word *ginggang*, meaning stripes, and the basic check made by stripes of woven color crossing each other on a white cotton ground has become a classic, used in countless contexts all over the world. The design is reproduced in all manner of colors and sizes, on silk taffetas and fine voiles, even painted on china. Although we tend to think of gingham in its simple country guise, it actually slips just as easily into sophisticated city surroundings. It is equally at home in a traditional kitchen, a children's den painted in bright primary colors, or a modern living room.

Gingham is the traditional folk fabric, the stuff of fresh peasant skirts and petticoats. In every French provincial village cottage windows are framed by red-and-white gingham curtains with a matching checked ruffle across the top, while the standard tablecloth used by French country restaurants and cafés is the traditional red gingham.

ABOVE: Gingham is a marvelously adaptable fabric for accessories, fitting cheerfully into a color scheme without overwhelming it. In the past, worn gingham petticoats were cut up and recycled as aprons, slipcovers and cushions, shoebags, lavender bags, and so on. Gingham is the decorator's cooking spice, added to ginger up quilts, or used in edgings to enliven plain fabrics.

LEFT: *We are used to seeing gingham curtains, but here a bold, red gingham check wallcovering has been used with great success in an urbane French-style drawing room. The toning pink sofa cover and window seat, and the patterned rug, add a muted effect that softens the walls.*

ABOVE: *Ginghams of different sizes can be combined with checks in similar colorways. The smaller-squared gingham is a favorite pattern for patchworks, as on the star cushion.*

RIGHT: *Clever curtain detailing marries different ginghams for the curtain and curtain support, and a third check for the grommet (eyelet) surrounds.*

While the French have made red gingham their own, the Scandinavians favor muted blues, greens, grays, and lilacs, which tone beautifully with off-white painted furniture and limed floors: imagine pale gingham-patterned silk taffeta curtains in a dove gray and white dining room. Bright blue gingham with traditional blue-and-white china, and yellow or white paintwork, is an unbeatable classic combination for an American or European country kitchen.

For those who like mixing patterns, gingham is an ideal component. One way to do this successfully is to mix larger and smaller check sizes in the same color, or alternatively you can use the same size check in contrasting colorways. Used for upholstery, the bigger checks can create a bold, formal look; gingham looks equally smart and well-dressed teamed with stripes of the same colorway; and it makes a delightful lining for floral curtains, combined in a matching colorway.

The main problem with all ginghams is to make sure that the lines match each other and run straight – unfortunately there is no secret solution, other than try, try, and try again!

FAR LEFT: The blue check fabric panel, with plain cream paintwork on the walls, creates a tailored contemporary version of the Scandinavian look, well suited to a bedroom.

LEFT: A cushion cover in outsize checks, with smart bow ties, is the well-dressed chair's dinner jacket.

Tartans

Rich, glowing tartans in woolen weaves have a totally different appeal from summery ginghams, despite the similarities in design. If you hanker after the Scots baronial look, tartans are definitely for you!

Legendarily worn by Scottish clans, early tartans were woven from yarn dyed with natural plants, mosses, and lichens in the muted colors of the Highlands – madder, ocher, heather, soft greens. A "plaid" was the length of tartan cloth flung over a shoulder and worn as a cape.

Along with other clannish customs, tartans were banned by the vengeful British for nearly a century, but enjoyed a revival in the nineteenth century, when clans often sported two tartans, one in subdued hues for hunting, and a brighter "dress" version for social events.

RIGHT: When teamed with soft blue, green, and pink, these tartan accessories take on a feminine feel.

LEFT: Small, jewel-bright tartan lampshades, for wall lights or candlestick lamps produce a cozy glow in a bedroom or living room.

ABOVE: Versatile tartan checks appear on everything from staircarpets and throws to handbags.

LEFT: A heap of scatter-cushions in contrasting tartans, linked by a dash of red, creates a warm and enticing hearthside welcome.

ABOVE: Black Watch, and its variations, are highly popular and found in the most unexpected contexts – as here, where the dark checks become a backdrop not for haggis but for a formal Japanese meal.

Queen Victoria had a passion for tartans, and her beloved Scottish home, Balmoral, was decked out with tartan walls, upholstery, and even carpets. A feature of Scottish castles and hunting lodges ever since, they have been successfully transplanted worldwide and are as much loved in Japan as in America.

Today's tartans are mostly made with artificially dyed yarns, so the colors are brighter. Their deep colors blend well with dark polished furniture, stone flags, and brick, and they are much in demand for studies and dens, or to warm up a living room, where the wool makes fine draft-excluding curtains for windows and doors. Like gingham, tartans are eminently adaptable, and their confident lines hold their own with stripes, brocades, and exotic paisleys.

LEFT: *The rich, heavy folds of a draped plaid make a warm, informal frame for deep windows and outward-opening French doors.*

BELOW LEFT: *Tailored finishes, like this curtain heading of smart yellow tabs and covered buttons, look especially good with tartans.*

BELOW RIGHT: *A tartan-effect paint treatment does wonders for a dining room.*

ABOVE: *A mundane kitchen cupboard is reincarnated in an outsize painted tartan, complete with cross-weave stripes, set against other checks, stripes, and vividly colored accessories.*

Bright Checks

Checked patterns in brazen colors are highly popular with home decorators, who revel in the exuberant effect of geometric pattern and primary colors. Modest cupboards and sideboards suddenly flaunt themselves in thoroughly modern oranges, reds, and yellows, the decorating equivalent of a clown's pair of outsize checked trousers. Giant window-pane checks in the brashest hues are splashed freehand over furniture and accessories in tongue-in-cheek homage to traditional tartans and ginghams.

While subtlety is not the name of the game here, nonetheless careful thought needs to be given to the colors you are combining, and the effect they will have on their surroundings. Displaying vivid checked furniture or soft furnishings against walls painted with dark, strong, flat, or broken color will balance their joky high spirits.

ABOVE: Cups and saucers, plates and jugs can be painted with a jolly, homemade checked effect to brighten up your breakfast.

RIGHT: Electrifying freehand paintwork transforms a nondescript cabinet with checks that are slyly reminiscent of old-fashioned carpet slippers. The dark walls roughly washed with blue and green echo the loosely finished effect.

Stripes

Striped wallpapers, paint treatments, and soft furnishings add instant sophistication to an interior. Formal or casual according to context, their simple geometric lines can pull together a color scheme, mix effortlessly with checks and patterns, and break up large areas of solid color on sofas or beds.

LEFT: *Blue and white is an especially pleasing partnership. These confident wall stripes in cerulean blue and white create a crisp, clean look.*

RIGHT: *Three different striped fabrics in the same colorway neatly contrast with the wall boarding.*

ABOVE: *Broad bands of two tones of green create a sophisticated look for dining room or study.*

ABOVE: *The handpainted finish enlivens these cheerful multicolored stripes.*

ABOVE: Vigorously contrasting yellow on white stripes effectively disguise marked walls.

ABOVE: Two shades of cream, ragged to add discreet texture, look quietly contemporary.

Striped Walls

Striped walls bring symmetry and order to rooms and passageways, evening out irregularities and adding height. Inch-wide Regency stripes in maroon or green and cream look elegant and formal with slender period furniture. Thin stripes, seen from a distance, tend to merge into a single color as a tactful coordinator with other patterns. Surface interest is added by wallpapers striped with satin and matte, or other contrasting textures in the same color. Wavy-edged stripes create a less regimented look. Stripes are also good at hiding marks and scratches – but make quite sure you start by getting them straight!

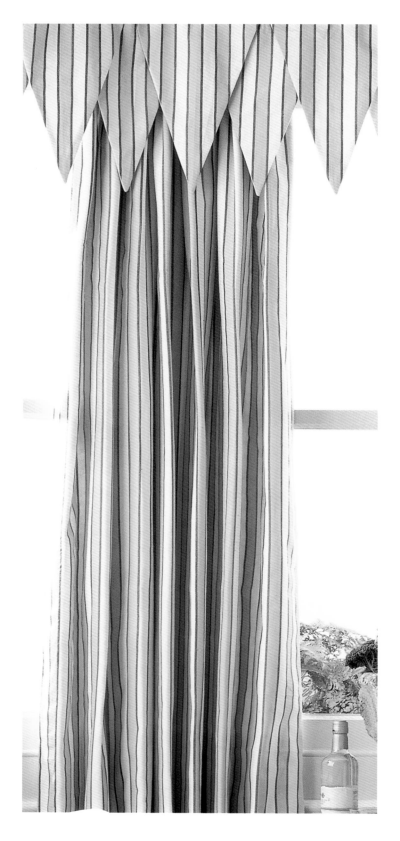

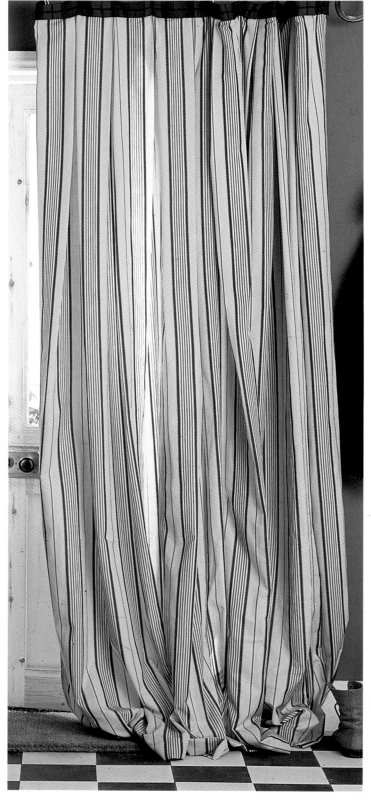

ABOVE: *The heightening effect of vertical stripes is emphasized by a harlequin valance.*

ABOVE: *A summery green and white cotton canvas is softly pleated for a door curtain.*

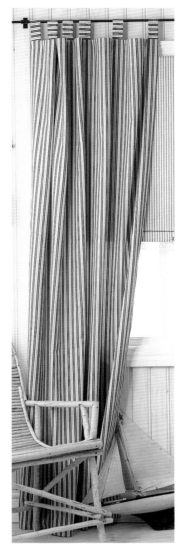

LEFT: This well-dressed window wears smart curtain tabs and a coordinated striped blind.

Striped Curtains

Stripes are an excellent choice for curtains. Simpler and less dominant than checks or complicated patterns, they also have a lighter effect than solid color. There is a huge variety of colors, weaves, patterns, and weights to choose from, from light, cheap cotton ticking to heavy brocades with a background stripe. Today's trend is to mix rather than match – the Long Island combination of cool stripes with chintzes and checks has become internationally popular. A lining of narrow stripes is charming for checked curtains, while a combination of toning, soft-colored stripes and checks is often used in Swedish style.

ABOVE: Horizontal stripes accentuate width; bright folk colors give a bold, exotic feel.

LEFT: *These dashing single curtains, cheaply made from strips of crisp navy and white cotton, add a dramatic focus to the double windows in a bedroom.*

Folk Story

Folk arts and crafts, with their vernacular roots and historical resonance, have become an enduring decorative inspiration. Plain walls and timber floors best display the unself-conscious charm of the beautifully made furniture, painted and stenciled finishes, quaint paintings, and domestic artifacts.

LEFT: *Form, pattern, and color are supplied by the delicately proportioned, traditionally painted furniture and decorative detail.*

RIGHT: *Samplers with lovingly embroidered improving verse have become family heirlooms.*

ABOVE: *A gold corn-ear motif is bold and effective stamped on a white jug and white-painted stool. Decorative stamping is one of the simplest of all paint techniques, adaptable to many different surfaces, and sits especially comfortably in a country-style kitchen.*

RIGHT: *A plain pine hutch (dresser) becomes a glowing work of art clad in stenciled fruit-and-flower and border motifs. Surroundings are important: subdued walls and blue-gray woodwork allow the paintwork its full glory.*

Painted Furniture

Decorated furniture was an especially strong element of American folk tradition, where many different European influences left their mark. Today's decorators cheerfully plunder inspiration from the painted pine of Scandinavia, colorful traditional designs from Russia, Mexico, and India, and Japanese and Chinese decorative finishes. Handpainted scenes, stylized, printed, or stenciled motifs, marbling, linework to edge or emphasize basic shape, dragging, stippling, and decoupage are all traditional decorating techniques. Some of these are highly skilled while others, like block printing and stenciling, are delightfully easy and enjoyable. Experiment, copy, or just collect as you please.

LEFT: The naive painted landscape continuing across the door panels transforms this wall cupboard into a picture in itself. A rough wash of deep blue over a terra-cotta base turns the cupboard into a dark, rustic frame. The rough-hewn finish can also look good in a contemporary room.

RIGHT: *Unbleached linen and cotton reps were traditional folk fabrics, decorated with tucks, drawn threadwork, smocking, piping, and other trimmings. The red repeat pattern on these cushions has been made with paint stamped on the fabric. A loose-weave throw adds color and texture.*

ABOVE: *Delicate miniature designs of leaves and flowers in russet, yellow, and green rest modestly on a cream or natural background.*

Fabric Charm

The simplicity and innocence of folk design has an informal appeal which is never outdated. The textiles characteristically combine stylized patterns with a small motif in two or three colors, limited in the past by the printing expense. Delicate Victorian flower sprigs, vivid French provincial cotton prints on a bright primary ground, and gingham checks are classics of the folk repertoire.

The fabrics look exquisite sewn into patchwork quilts, whose designs have themselves been the inspiration for today's textile designers. Rustic burlap (hessian), antique linen, printed or painted canvas and muslin (calico), and cross-stitch embroidery can all be incorporated into this decorative folk story. Use the finer weaves and designs with furniture on a similar delicate scale, like slender chairs with a well-crafted finish, and the rougher textiles with robust settles and cupboards for a more homespun look.

ABOVE: Crisp red-and-white gingham acquires folk art appeal with a sweetheart motif stamped on some of the white squares – a charming variation on a classic country look for kitchen or bedroom.

LEFT: *A fine collection of folk art and crafts adapts timelessly to a modern loft, against a neutral background of white walls, cream sofa, and marquetry floor. Evocative, handcrafted furniture is spare and sculptural, while the toy horses displayed on the table have a poignant simplicity.*

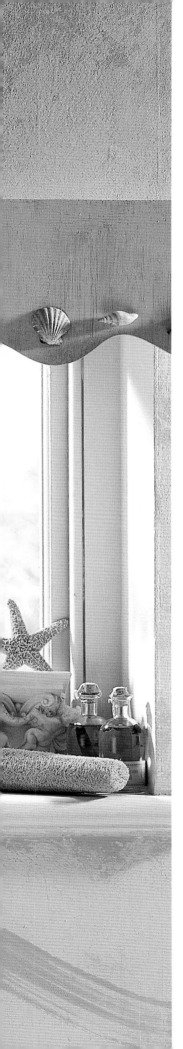

Sea Style

Marine themes have a special place in the decorator's repertoire. The seaside is ever-popular, while boats and shells, and fish and starfish make pretty, stylish design motifs, and there is something tranquil and restful about the thought of far blue horizons. All you have to do is take the plunge . . .

LEFT: Make waves with an aqueous blue wash; an undulating waterline beneath the window echoes the cornice (pelmet) above, with its cockleshells all in a row.

RIGHT: Iridescent-scaled, streamlined fish are favorite marine subjects.

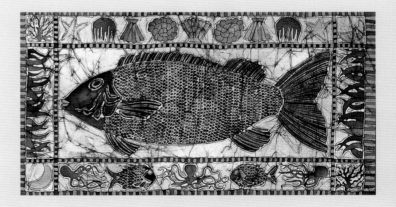

Marine Bathrooms

The bathroom is the ideal place for a marine theme, making bathtime feel like a holiday. When gathering your ideas for a seaside look, think back to your last visit to the sea and remember the colors – blues, grays, aquamarine, turquoise – the briny spray, and the patterns made by waves. Then there are the clapboard houses, and the wooden decks with deckchairs in faded striped canvas. Brightly painted boats with their rigging and ensigns bob in the harbor, and fishermen's nets and coils of rope lie on the quay. And underwater are the multitude of marine creatures, with their strange shapes and colors . . .

To achieve the effect, watery blue washes in different shades and hues are a good paint treatment, or splash out with really color-saturated blues and blue-greens, teamed either with dazzling white or with sandy, seashore colors. Keep your basic scheme simple, using hues of similar brightness, or one color in different tones; then the addition of seashore accessories will complete the style, rather than becoming messy and over-indulgent.

FAR LEFT: Strong "waves" of similar-toned blue and green, alternating with white, create a lighthearted ocean-going atmosphere – not for the queasy!

LEFT: The sand-and-sea theme is heightened by the humorous crab and fish stenciling. Wooden boarding makes a practical backsplash for bath and basin, allowing standing room for beach mementoes on top.

OPPOSITE: Seaside and fishy accessories create instant marine style for little outlay.

Beach Interiors

The houses of the Hamptons and the New England coastline have bequeathed a distinctive decorating style that suits many countries and climates. This cool, airy look instantly evokes summer by the sea: sunwashed rooms with cream or white walls, and open windows with voile or cotton curtains billowing in the sea breeze.

Floors are bleached, painted, or limewashed boards, covered by rag rugs or seagrass matting. Interiors are simply furnished with white or natural wickerwork, scrubbed kitchen tables, blue-painted cupboards, and kitchen chairs. Sail-canvas blinds match the sun-faded plain colors or cheerful stripes of comfortably upholstered sofas and daybeds. Steamer chairs, canvas-covered directors' chairs, and folding tables can be carried outside for sunbathing. Storage chests, antiqued or painted with seascapes, can stow away sailing gear to keep the place shipshape.

Walls clad with painted tongue-and-groove boards look neat and nautical. To complete the scene, meals are served on robust pottery in cheerful colors, on a gingham or oilcloth-covered table, and supper is lit by seagoing yacht lamps, or candles sheltering in lanterns.

RIGHT: Sand and white have been chosen for this unusual warm, sunny alternative to blues and greens. Unbleached muslin (calico), enlivened by simple stamped or stenciled starfish and scallop-shell motifs, is used to cover a screen and padded storage boxes, and sewn into a shoebag.

RIGHT: *Seashore foragers turn driftwood, bleached and washed by the waves, into dramatic sculpted frames for seascapes, sepia photographs, and mirrors. Rope, shells, pebbles, fishermen's cork floats, and other flotsam and jetsam can all be ingredients for decorative frames.*

BELOW: *Shutters and bedside cupboard are painted soft marine blue and distressed to look weathered, and a watery blue wash on the walls continues the theme. Below the chair rail dotted Swiss (spotted voile) and net are decoratively gathered and tied to add a fresh, feminine feature to a seaside bedroom.*

Crisp, clean bedlinen with a nautical trim, striped pillowcases with their neat buttoned finish, and honeycomb-textured towels make a coastal cottage bedroom shipshape. Add pale blue-green walls and furniture with a sea-washed paint effect for quintessential seaside style.

RIGHT: A papier mâché dish acquires three-dimensional drama with shells made of modeling clay glued to the rim. Gorgeous tropical fish complete the dish's subterranean splendor.

ABOVE AND BELOW: Barnacles, cockles, and snail shells supply the designs for a charming tablecloth embroidered in shades of aquamarine and sand.

Seashore Details

The more restrained you have been with your basic marine decor, the more you can go to town – or rather, to sea – with your accessories. The ocean and all its exotic and strange inhabitants await your inspiration. Wonderfully multifarious tropical fish of all shapes and sizes can float past on your plates and dishes, and flaunt their finny forms on wall plaques. Scour thrift shops for fish-shaped pottery plates of the 1920s and 1930s; cheap glass fish dishes are made by French manufacturers today; or have fun making your own decorative versions with papier mâché.

Booty from seashore walks can be turned into decorating treasure. Shells and coral, bleached by sea and sun, have their own unmatched beauty (but never break off coral, which takes centuries for its minute living inhabitants to rebuild). Shell decoration has enjoyed a tongue-in-cheek revival; arrange, then

LEFT: The stylized geometric shapes of shells are versatile stenciling and stamping motifs, used here on tiles, a blue-painted cigar box, and a drawstring bag. A simple repeat pattern of sailing boats is also bright and effective. Gold and silver highlights have a special affinity with blue.

ABOVE AND BELOW: Fanciful fish, mermaids, sea-horses, and sea-dragons have decorated maps, textiles, and tapestries for centuries. The strong lines and colors of fish, here adapted to wall plaques and a fishy box, make wonderful accessories in a marine-style bathroom.

glue your seaside finds (or recycled shells from the seafood store) around a mirror or picture, to cover boxes, or even to adorn a fireplace. Large shells can be displayed on windowsill or mantelshelf for a natural look; small ones can be piled together in a dish, or in a glass jar filled with water to bring out their iridescent colors. The same can be done with smooth, rounded pebbles, which on a larger scale serve as handsome weights for papers, or as doorstops. Jewel-bright blue and green "angel's tears," tiny glass "pebbles" buffed and smoothed by the sea, look exquisite in a molded white or clear glass dish.

Seaweed, shells, and fish are traditional decorative motifs in folk art: wavy-legged blue octopi on Greek vases and jugs, for instance. A painted and stenciled galvanized metal or enamel bucket makes a good wastepaper basket. Enamel mugs, stamped with a simple marine design, make practical kitchenware. Loops of ships' rope or cord are threaded with shells or painted cork fishing weights for nicely nautical curtain tiebacks.

Traditional Style

This comfortable, welcoming style is easy to live with, if not always so easy to achieve. The ingredients of traditional style seem to have been put together over time apparently at random, though it was probably carefully planned. Its relaxed, uncontrived mixture of pattern and texture are keynotes.

LEFT: *This inviting living room is warmed by strong terra-cotta walls and assorted red-patterned textiles, with touches of complementary green.*

RIGHT: *Mix, not match – contrasting patterns, bright colors – is the guiding motto.*

Patterned Decoration

Pattern combined with color defines traditional style. The aim is to make it look as natural as possible, whether you are using painted designs, textiles, or both. With traditional techniques like stenciling, there is no harm in following the early color combinations which have stood the test of time. Stenciled effects used red with green or indigo blue and black on a creamy ground, or pale colors on a red base.

Layers of textiles can be added in unstudied profusion, in the form of throws and cushions, enriched by braids, tassels, trimmings, and oriental rugs. Mixing patterns is quite an art, and experimenting is essential. Rules are made to be broken, but a good starting point is to mix patterns in toning colors, or that are roughly on the same scale.

RIGHT: *Pattern profusion is controlled by color use. Red and gold textiles are complemented by antique gold finishes, and a deep red-brown chest.*

ABOVE: *Toning striped ticking works with kilim-print curtains because both patterns are geometric, and small stripes or checks merge at a distance.*

LEFT: *Country weds traditional in this classic family kitchen, with its Aga range, assorted crockery on display, wicker baskets, and carver chair.*

RIGHT: *Traditional red-and-cream toile de Jouy, popular since the eighteenth century, is the base for this ravishingly pretty living room. The original design is repeated on the wallpaper. Toning checked and striped cottons contrast with the main theme, without dominating it.*

ABOVE: Tudor-style tapestry cushions sit well with dark polished oak.

Traditional Fabrics

Traditional style thrives on variety, especially where textiles are concerned. Choosing fabrics can be the most enjoyable part of decorating; but the enormous array of designs and finishes to choose from today can be positively bewildering. The answer is, when mixing textiles, to go for fabrics of a similar character and weight. Or hunt for antique or period curtains, or lovely fragments for cushions. Earlier designers rinsed brand-new chintzes in tea to give them a fashionably faded look.

OPPOSITE: Magnificent brocades, damasks, velvets, antique embroideries, tassels, and braids, draped and massed together, create a fabulously opulent atmosphere. These grand designs are redolent of grand rooms made for grand living. Antique textiles are beautiful, but fragile and light-sensitive.

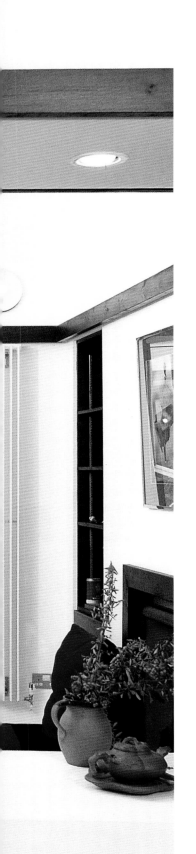

Cool and Minimal

If traditional style depends for effect on adding pattern, texture, and depth, the minimal look is all about subtraction. Color is flat, white or neutral, furniture reduced to a functional minimum. Architecture is all-important and all-controlling, supplying harmony in design, structure, and space.

LEFT: *Form is function in this cool, Modernist living area where decoration is all in the design.*

RIGHT: *The elegant simplicity of this tableware is designed to display the food it serves.*

Graphic Walls

Minimalism is a way of life, easier to aspire to than to attain. Minimal is radical, effective, stylish – and ruthless. It relies on cutting out all distracting or superfluous decoration. On a clean, empty wall the design of a radiator becomes crucial, while a single painting, sculpture, or vase is a visual feast. It is eminently suited to busy, twentieth-century city life because its firm lines, clutter-free corners, and smooth surfaces require minimum maintenance.

This look is highly controlled, and when it depends on built-in, site-specific structural features dedicated to function, it can be unexpectedly ill-adapted to, say, the messiness of family life. But in an age devoted to consumerism, minimalism's almost monastic simplicity can bring peace of mind through an aesthetic of purity and efficiency recalling an oriental austerity.

In this soothingly bare environment, walls are of graphic importance and detail is crucial. Lines are sharply squared off or rectilinear, abolishing cozy curves. Wall surfaces may be smooth plaster or raw brick; paints are clean whites and creams, sometimes partnered with black gloss for dramatic emphasis. White walls need to be refreshed regularly to look good, but this is easily done in minimalist surroundings. Pictures or other decorative features must be exceptionally carefully hung, since the effect depends on razor-sharp symmetry.

RIGHT: *Two rows of exactly spaced dark blue tiles on clean white walls bring a sense of well-ordered symmetry to a modern kitchen.*

OPPOSITE: *The geometric simplicity of regularly spaced squares is sharply defined, pleasingly proportioned, and stylish.*

OPPOSITE FAR RIGHT: *A black radiator acquires sculptural status against a backdrop of cool, clear blue. Black-and-white prints complement the pared-down, contemporary look.*

LEFT: *Less is more in this emphatically interesting monochrome bathroom with geometric checkerboard tiles. The reclaimed bath and reproduction shower are teamed with contemporary black and white to create a timeless modern look, relying on carefully judged proportions for its effect.*

A Limited Palette

A softer version of minimal style allows a slightly more extended, though still limited, color palette, and more room for texture and decorative detail. This is a controlled but sensuous look, relying on splashes of solid color and a few well-crafted pieces of furniture.

Concentrate on good quality that will last. If you can afford it, honey-colored varnished floorboards lighten your living space and are a classically good-looking base: a cream wash under varnish gives an extra-pale look. Coir, sisal, or seagrass matting is a pale neutral, durable alternative. Walls might be creams teamed with caned colonial or leather furniture in shades of brown, with touches of ethnic pattern. Or start with white and add color: white and pale gray walls with lime green or yellow, or white with dashes of madder red or indigo textiles. Fabrics include linen, cotton, jute, muslin, and wool, in plain colors or stripes.

Furniture may be from various periods or different continents, if assembled with panache – such as a carved Indian coffee table with a calico sofa, enlivened by bright cushions. Architectural stonework or plaster details are salvaged to become sculptural living room features.

Contemporary and comfortable to live with, this style looks a million dollars, and sometimes costs it, but with the use of clever coordination you can achieve the effect for very much less.

LEFT: Whitewashed walls with painted wood and plain linen contrive this simple, well-composed look which is both pared down and decorative.

ABOVE RIGHT: White or cream flowers are the ultimate accessory for the understated look: pretty, fresh, and cool, with the attractive contrast of the rough, weathered terra-cotta pot.

RIGHT: Efficient white tiles for the kitchen work surface and backsplash are enlivened by a bas-relief frieze of tiles.

LEFT: *Minimal white walls and stained floorboards are given a modern facelift of fashionable acid-green paintwork. The curved sides of the white-painted beds repeat the lines of the slender stool legs. Soft furnishings provide interest with stripes and neat, tailored, toning edgings.*

RIGHT: Spiky grasses and bamboos are the architectural statements of the plant world. Their elegant outlines are cool, fresh, and modern, especially when offset by no-nonsense galvanized metal buckets rather than earthenware or ceramics.

BELOW: Window blinds take up less space, let in more light, and are usually cheaper than curtains – and they are often quite easy to make. A classic stripe looks smart and uncluttered in colors tied in with the rest of the room.

Elegant Details

If you yearn for minimal style but your time or your funds won't stretch to a complete domestic makeover, you can still find ways to introduce the look. Remember that the equation depends mainly on what you can take out. The illusion of space is the ultimate luxury in today's acquisitive society. Strip your furniture and possessions down to the bare essentials and throw out what you don't need – you'll be amazed at the junk you have been storing when you start sorting it all out.

A strictly no-frills attitude is required when it comes to decorative extras. An object's decorative value should be intrinsic to its design and use; wherever possible, choose the purely practical over the ornamental. If you are introducing pattern in textiles, geometric, contemporary, or ethnic is preferable; interest can be added with decorative bindings and edgings. Go for natural materials and pure colors. A glass vase of tulips, a row of pebbles or shells on the mantelpiece, a collection of carved wooden spoons hung on the wall are effortlessly stylish and within almost any budget.

LEFT: *Where decorative interest is added, it needs to be geometric and simple. A calligraphic trim of matching ribbon is stitched onto a plain cream blind, outlining the cutout shape at the bottom, to take it out of the ordinary. Light flooding in from outside emphasizes the design.*

ABOVE: *Graphic silhouettes in a painted frame are bold and effective.*

DECORATING WITH SOFT FURNISHINGS

Introduction

Soft furnishings, the all-important clothes of a room, give the key to its function and mood. Textiles of every kind – stiff, supple, rough or smooth, plain or printed, woven, knitted, or sewn – contribute to the final effect of a room. Plush velvets for a cozy sitting room, crisp twills for a businesslike study, or chic dining room table linen, textiles cover and complete, they dress up or disguise, invite you to touch, or quite simply look wonderful.

LEFT: *Neat tailored fabrics in fresh greens and white, lifted with splashes of yellow, give this room a light and airy feel.*

RIGHT: *A formal polished dining table, set for dinner. is given delicacy and flair with fine embroidered linen and a deft twist of grosgrain (petersham) ribbons.*

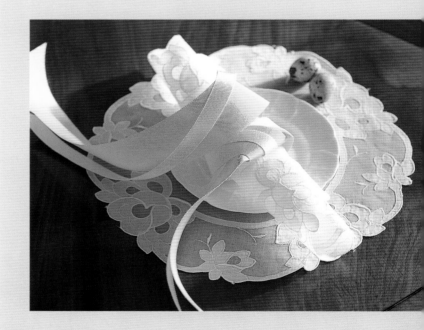

Fabric Textures and Weaves

When choosing fabrics, it is important to consider the effect of texture and weave. Plain and firmly woven fabrics have strength and a smooth, solid appearance; uneven yarns, such as slubbed silks or natural homespun cottons, may be as strong, but their less regular surface is pleasingly varied. Damasks and brocades combine weave patterns to make richly textured fabrics with lustrous highlights. Velvets both reflect and absorb light, depending on how it strikes the fabric's pile, suggesting warmth and depth.

LEFT: Laces and nets in natural or metallic threads can be used on their own for light, dappled effects, or laid over heavier, colorful fabric to stunning effect. Fine-meshed nets are very good for multiple layering; larger-patterned laces make excellent curtains for screening without darkening.

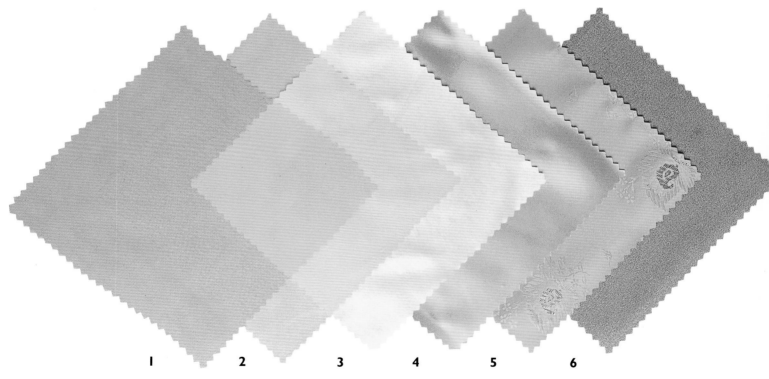

1   2   3   4   5   6

ABOVE: Silk is available in a vast range of textures, from heavy brocades, often incorporating metallic threads, to feather-light chiffon. All have that indefinable luster of luxury, and all can be awkward to work. Use fine needles, pins, and thread and be generous with seam allowances. Baste everything, and press with a cool iron as you work.

1 Chiffon: airy, matte, translucent. 2 Organza: gauzy, sleek. 3 Thai silk: subtle, uneven texture. 4 Heavy satin: luxurious, smooth sheen. 5 Brocade: figured, lively surface. 6 Satin: rich, softly shimmering fabric.

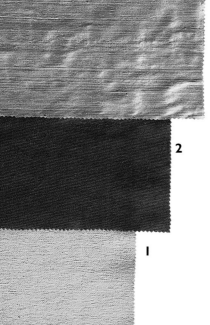

4

3

5

6

7

LEFT AND ABOVE: *Formal fabrics, heavy and richly textured, suggest wonderful luxury. Often used for a period feel, cut velvets, damasks, and chenille make opulent curtains and covers, embellished with cords and tassels. Sumptuous and durable, velvet and moleskin are supreme for upholstery and slipcovers, teamed with shot silk or embroidered cushions.*

1 *Chenille: uneven double-sided pile, very soft, drapes well.* **2** *Moleskin: soft, velvety, tough.* **3** *Indian dupion silk: striking, shot (two-tone) slubbed fabric.* **4** *Crewel-work: hand-embroidered, wool on heavy cotton.* **5** *Velvet: smoother than chenille, richer than moleskin.* **6** *Cut velvet: raised pattern.* **7** *Damask: contrasting textures in weave pattern.*

2

1

ABOVE: *All in plain weave, these linens show the subtle variations of color and texture in natural fabrics.*

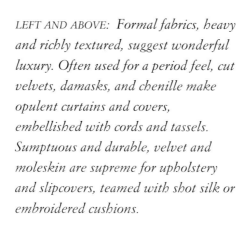

5

6

4

3

7

2

1

LEFT AND ABOVE: *Informal fabrics are functional, and have strong, individual character. They give a practical, contemporary air to a room.*
1 *Burlap (hessian): rough, dramatic.*
2 *Indian handloomed cotton: uneven.*
3 *Corduroy: soft, hardwearing.* **4** *Linen hopsack: distinctive.* **5** *Herringbone tweed: raw silk; drapes beautifully.* **6** *Canvas: strong.* **7** *Linen union: tough.*

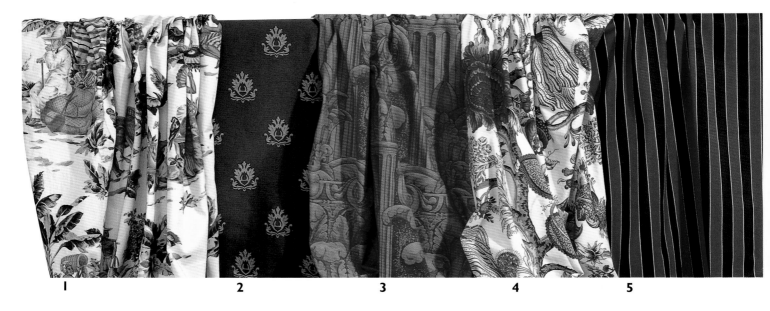

1   2   3   4   5

Fabric Patterns

Printed or woven, pattern forms a powerful visual texture. Large patterns are striking and emphatic, demanding space and attention, while small overall patterns give the illusion of a single, if broken, color.

ABOVE: **1** *Beautifully printed, bold, overall pattern, uses a wide range of colors.* **2** *Striking woven motif, gold on green.* **3** *Large, dramatic pattern; best used flat for full impact.* **4** *Lively chintz drapes well for curtains.* **5** *Uncompromising stripes woven in supple wool; rich and soft.*

LEFT: Small prints in coordinated colors unify a color scheme. These prints each share two or more of three principal colors – navy, red, and cream. Common colors ensure harmony despite the variety of patterns.

RIGHT: Prints in either light or dark tones of a single color, even with other colors added, also harmonize, provided that there is a constant theme, as here, red and burgundy.

BELOW AND RIGHT: **1** *Woven motif: good with harmonious colors.* **2** *Floral print: Eastern influence, bold, richly colored.* **3** *Ethnic print: robust, warm, earthy.* **4** *Figurative print: panel design could be divided.* **5** *Woven stripe: bold, balances other designs.* **6** *Plaid: unites disparate colors in a scheme.*

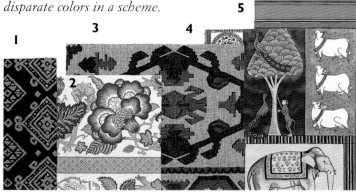

LEFT AND BELOW: **1** *Gingham check: coordinates with geometric patterns.* **2** *Narrow stripe: like plain fabric, coordinates well.* **3** *Toile de Jouy: classic monochrome print.* **4** *Abstract print: large, subtle.* **5** *Small print: effective with geometrics.* **6** *Repeated pattern: woven, ideal for upholstery.*

RIGHT: *Most chintzes and figurative designs, and inexpensive geometric patterns, are printed on the right side of fabric, while tartans, tweeds, and ginghams are woven. Patterns must be carefully matched to achieve a professional finish.*

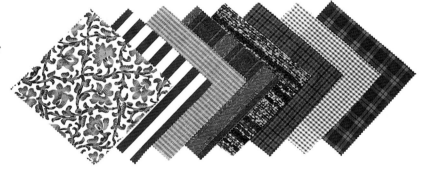

BELOW: **1** *Bold tartan demands flamboyant use.* **2** *Shimmering figured velvet.* **3** *A striking weave for dramatic surroundings.* **4** *Colorful Madras suits curtains.* **5** *Vivid stripes make a dynamic blind.*

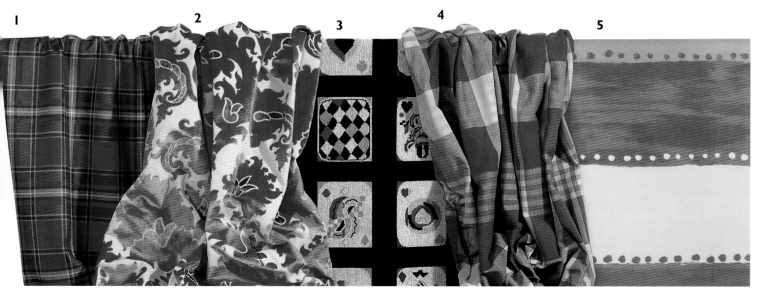

Combining Colors

Color is probably the first thing to be noticed in any decorative scheme. Some colors simply seem right together while others always look uncomfortable. The whole mood of a room can be radically altered by changing its overall color emphasis, making it appear warm and welcoming, or cool, clean, and fresh.

The key to color harmony is to recognize compatible groupings of colors. Warm colors, yellows through orange and red to purple, appear to advance toward the viewer, whereas cool colors, acid yellows through green and blue to violet, appear to recede. Using one warm color with a group of cool colors, or vice versa, gives a dramatic lift to a color scheme.

Darkening or lightening color exaggerates its spatial effect, so pale blue will seem to increase space and distance in a room, whereas deep red-purple will make a room appear much smaller and more intimate. Close tones or colors are more restful than strong contrasts.

Soft furnishings provide one of the easiest ways of changing the color balance in a room. The addition of a few scatter cushions, or a new tablecloth or bedspread can transform the color scheme to dramatic effect.

ABOVE: Cool colors in close tones combine well, accented by warm pink and red of similar tonal value.

RIGHT: The quilt uses the same colors as the fabric samples above. Lighter than the background, the central motif stands out in this rich color scheme successfully mixing warm and cool colors.

ABOVE: *An inviting tumble of warm, toning cushions, shimmering softly with gold.*

LEFT: *Subdued colors in closely related hues have a restrained, sophisticated feel.*

RIGHT: *Dark, almost black, colored linen is complemented by broad, dark orange, grosgrain (petersham) ribbons.*

Mixing Texture, Pattern, and Color

The cornucopia of color, pattern, and texture found in textiles offers tremendous
opportunities for mixing fabrics in exciting combinations. Blend rough silk dupions with
heathery tweed; set off the stiffness of a sharply tailored sofa with embroidered cushions
glittering with metallic threads; combine printed chintzes in a riot of floral, figurative, and
geometric patterns; or set sleek satin and velvet against smooth, translucent muslin drapes.

The accompanying cast of trimmings, braids, ribbons, tassels, and bows add detail and
focus to the repertoire, but remember there should be one common feature between
different fabrics used together whether it be texture, pattern, color, or tone.

ABOVE: *Fringes, tassels, lace and braid, buttons and bows, in silk, wool, and metal thread: these are all ways of adding extra interest to cushions and giving their edges definition.*

RIGHT: *Bold printed curtains, pleated into formal headings, have here been enlivened with lighthearted bows made from bright red yarn.*

RIGHT: *Contrasting tweeds, one rugged and one smooth, are united with bias binding in blue picked out from the checks.*

Curtains and Blinds

From grand, layered drapes with valances or swags to simple shades in cotton, curtains and blinds create drama and focus in any room. They frame the windows, linking the interior with the outdoor view. Stylishly and effectively, curtains provide privacy and insulation from the cold.

LEFT: *Secured with heavy tassels, this figured curtain hung from a brass pole makes a dramatic focal point to any room.*

RIGHT: *A stark wrought-iron rod with rings admirably suits this elegant cream and dark green striped curtain, loosely pleated into a simple tartan heading.*

Traditional Patterns

Using fabrics either printed or woven in traditional patterns makes a room feel comfortable and familiar. Floral motifs have always been particularly popular for furnishings, and there is a huge variety of styles, from blowzy roses arranged haphazardly through to naive bouquets and formal, regular designs.

Given the relatively large area occupied by curtains, an uncomplicated treatment works well with traditional patterns. Changing the scale of the design, for use on cushions for instance, or using it in a different form, such as embroidery, adds interest without overpowering a room. As long as they have colors in common, a mixture of patterns can work well, though some coordination helps to maintain an atmosphere of calm.

ABOVE: *Prints in the same colors but in different sizes work well together. Light, fresh colors look good with old, well-polished wood.*

LEFT: *Large flowers on dusty pink, these curtains make the room look comfortable, calm, and welcoming.*

OPPOSITE: *The strong repeat of this William Morris print is well displayed and complemented by the needlepoint versions on the chair seats and cushion.*

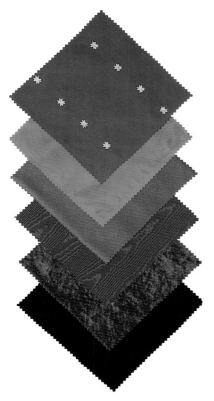

ABOVE: Some synthetic fabrics in various blues; embroidered polyester, woven polyester, Lycra, moiré taffeta, and crushed and woven velvet.

ABOVE: Vinyl offers a smooth surface like leather or suede; use as a foil to woven and knitted textiles.

Cool Blues

Decorating rooms in shades of single colors gives them distinctive character. Blue is a cool, fresh color which suggests space and serenity. Its clean quality may make it seem cold, but it can be warmed or lifted by other colors in a scheme. It works very well with white, looking brilliant in checks and stripes, but can be successfully "dirtied" if you want to create a more subtle effect.

Because of its associations with water, blue is a favorite color for kitchens and bathrooms, but it is eminently suitable for any room where impressions of spaciousness and tranquility are required.

LEFT: *This soft blue and cream striped curtain is given a deep matching valance trimmed with thick cotton rope; a pretty but subtle and sophisticated treatment.*

BELOW: *Cool blue fabrics, prints, and weaves.* **1** *Crisp poplin: use for blinds and curtains.* **2** *Classic cotton checks.* **3** *Chintz: old style, charming.* **4** *Inky midnight velvet: makes luxurious curtains.* **5** *Fresh tricolor checks: good for curtains or blinds.*

OPPOSITE: *Curving crests machined into this brilliant blue curtain are cut roughly to reveal turquoise waves; the seashore cornice (pelmet) is shaped and colorwashed hardboard, littered with washed-up seashells.*

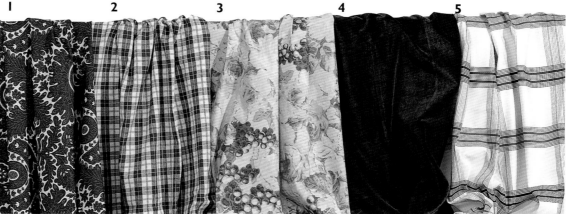

Using Heading Tape

You can use heading tape to make a plain pencil pleat heading, creating a simple but elegant curtain that allows the fabric to show off its charms. Use good lining fabric and interlining for added insulation if necessary and allow enough fabric for a generous hem. Heading tape usually comes with tips on how much fabric you will need.

1 Measure finished length; mark; cut off lining and interlining, not main fabric.

2 Fold over hem; turn in top edge and corners; pin in place.

3 Machine heading tape in place, folding under ends; leave cords free at one end.

4 Draw up cords to desired width; tie, do not cut. Insert hook in every fourth pocket.

Hot Reds

Red is the ultimate comfort color. Soft, deep, and enveloping, it makes a room look inviting and intimate. Rusty reds tinged with brown convey richness and old-world grandeur. Clear cherry red is young and dynamic.

Such a positive color can sometimes be difficult to team with others, but colors of the same degree of brightness will harmonize. As with any strong color, white contrasts well, and red with black makes for a punchy effect. Otherwise you can use it sparingly to introduce dashes of warmth into an otherwise cool-colored interior.

BELOW: Checks in warm earthy colors and pale gold enhance brick red walls.

LEFT: *For a child's room, bright red and white checks make cheerful curtains, with a button-trimmed tab heading.*

Making a Tab Heading

Tab headings are simple and effective sewn headings for ungathered curtains. Their easy drape and lack of fuss is ideal for informal rooms, adding interest without being in any way overpowering.

Tabs can be plain, made in self fabric as here, or dressed up with a contrasting fabric and fancy buttons.

1 Cut card template to finished tab size; draw around template centered on stripe, on wrong side of fabric; cut out with ⅝in (1.5cm) seam allowance.

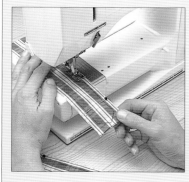

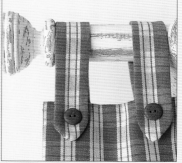

2 Right sides together, stitch two pieces along template marking; leave straight end open.

3 Cut away fabric close to seam, leaving ¹⁄₁₆in (2mm) allowance.

4 Turn tabs right side out, helping corners with scissors; press.

5 Sew straight end onto back of curtain; fasten pointed end to the front with a button.

Translucent Window Treatments

Sometimes curtains are needed to give privacy but not to exclude light. Muslin, organza, and tulle are all lightweight, translucent fabrics, which give screening without making a room too dark during the day. They are also inexpensive, so they can be used extravagantly with great dramatic effect.

Sheer fabrics can be plain or figured, in natural or synthetic yarns. Cottons and silks drape a little more softly than synthetics, which can be rather slippery.

ABOVE: Plain and printed viscose, and plain organza: colored and filmy white voile can be overlaid to create layered effects in subtle dappled color.

ABOVE RIGHT: Loosely woven gauze is an inexpensive window veil, here made special by stamping it with a simple motif, echoed on the cornice (pelmet).

RIGHT: Soft, diffused sunlight shines through a ripple of striped organza hung from a thin rod. A sewn casing makes the simple heading.

OPPOSITE: Accompanied by stark, dramatic furniture, clouds of fine white muslin are stapled above the window, then draped and loosely knotted for instant glamor.

Simple Blinds

Where space around the window is restricted, or a neat uncluttered treatment is required, simple panel blinds provide an elegant solution. They consist of rectangular panels of fabric, drawn up into folds with cords threaded through vertical rows of rings. Panel blinds are easy and inexpensive to make, because they need less fabric than any other type of window covering, and almost all fabrics are suitable. They can also act as a private art gallery; fabric featuring large prints, especially portraits, looks uniquely impressive.

Suitable fabrics can be used to make effective light-filtering blinds for very sunny rooms, perhaps to be hung in conjunction with more ornate curtains. Decorative hems add interest. Nevertheless, the stylish simplicity of panel blinds is particularly suitable where ornament would be inappropriate; their look is supremely modern.

RIGHT: A striped blind, bordered with rusty red, is set inside the window frame. The stripes echo the reeded wood trim.

OPPOSITE: This airy room is awash with light filtered through creamy-pale blinds, each drawn to a different height, all linked decoratively with a swag of thick rope.

ABOVE: Chevrons cut into the hem follow the design of the fabric print.

ABOVE: A scalloped edge for a pretty floral blind.

ABOVE: Toning colored tassels adorn the bottom of the blind.

ABOVE: Doubled fabric, smartly box-pleated, and sewn on below the casing.

Decorative Blinds

By altering the way in which they are corded, blinds can be made to look very decorative. As with panel blinds, cords are threaded through rings on the back of the blind. The fabric is flounced and gathered into billows, or folded into pleats.

The relaxed look of decorative blinds is easy to live with; they can serve as decorative fixed screens rather than functioning, lifting blinds, and while some styles are elaborate, perhaps fussy, with robust materials and jolly prints, lighthearted "fun" versions can be made using the same techniques.

RIGHT: *Rolled up and fastened with silk ties, this elegant taffeta blind is used as a permanent screen.*

Cording a Blind

Cords for simple decorative blinds run through two vertical rows of rings sewn to the back of the blind. A lath is attached to the top of the blind, with a screw eye fitted above each row of rings. Cords are threaded upwards from the bottom ring and then one cord is also taken through the screw eye so that the cords hang together at one side.

1 *Sew rings 4in (10cm) from sides of blind at 12in (30cm) intervals.*

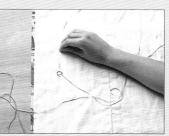

2 *Thread cords through rings and screw eye; gather cords to one side.*

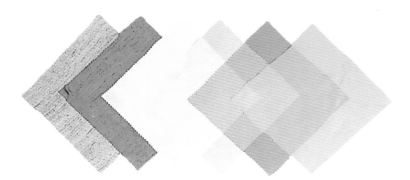

A Natural Look

Perhaps as a reaction to the hurly-burly of modern life, the gently bleached colors and pleasing textures of natural materials create a mood of easy calm.

Fabrics with distinctive or random textures, such as slubbed silks, or burlap (hessian) and linen, are particularly attractive in a natural color scheme. A limited palette of neutral or earthy colors brings out the qualities of soft and hard furnishings. Walls painted in faded creams, waxed wooden furniture, delicate country china, all are set off and flattered by soft unbleached muslin, coarse linen, or rustling tussah silk.

ABOVE: *Honey and sand; shimmering tussah silk; amber dupion; satin, pearl-shadowed with habotai; cloudy organza and chiffon.*

RIGHT: *Creamy seersucker, bunched in a tieback of homespun cotton decorated with pearl buttons.*

OPPOSITE: *Ripples of seagrass beachmat, trimmed with burlap (hessian) and gold stars, complimenting cinnamon walls and a stripped pine door.*

Tiebacks

As well as purpose-made cords and tassels, almost anything can be used for tiebacks as long as it holds the curtains back from the window.

Themed ready-mades can be used to imaginative effect; braided raffia in a garden room; old school neckties for a study; harness in a horse-mad child's room.

Formal, understated, or witty and exuberant, tiebacks allow for fun as well as function.

ABOVE: A pretty garland of ivy; plastic strands and printed fabric is wired to entwine around a heavy lace curtain.

ABOVE RIGHT: Coordinating checks with sunflower petal points attached to the lower hem, fastened through with a casual knot for fresh, country chic.

RIGHT: Rich, heavyweight, silky tassels and bullion fringe adorn an opulent, traditional brocade curtain against a formal, striped wall.

LEFT: *Simple but stylish; braided cast-offs make a rope in blues which match the woven curtain fabric.*

BELOW: *Clean, old, knitted wool and cotton garments, dyed and braided together to make a thick soft rope with a wonderful nubbly texture.*

Making Tiebacks

To work out how much fabric you need, first measure around the curtain where the tieback will be. Draw a long oval to this length. Cut two pieces of fabric to this shape, allowing ⅝ in (1.5cm) seam allowance all around. These will be joined with right sides together, leaving a gap in the seam for turning, to make one tieback.

1 *Sew front and back together; turn right side out; hand sew the gap; press.*

2 *Sew ring at each end; fasten onto hooks screwed into the wall.*

Top Treatments

An interesting or unusual top treatment can really liven up a room. Tabs, continuous ropes or tapes, and ties are all effective ways of hanging plain curtains from poles. For more formal and elaborate curtains there are many different heading tapes available, enabling various patterns of pleating and gathering, all easy to use.

Complex headings in matching or contrasting fabrics add an impressive finishing touch; much work, but well worth the effort for the final result and very useful for hiding unsightly rods.

OPPOSITE: Ribbon bows are tied over a plain wooden pole for an almost flat curtain of charming simplicity.

RIGHT: Three bold, luscious colors make a stunning modern version of a classic draped valance.

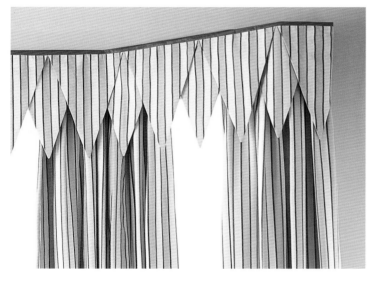

ABOVE: Layered chevrons edged with braid make an elegant cornice (pelmet) for tall windows.

LEFT: A formal goblet pleat heading is here enriched with a heavy fringe.

RIGHT: Snappy fringe, rickrack, and ribbon make a striking accompaniment for a plain curtain.

ABOVE: A beach-bleached bathroom curtain is given the Midas touch with gold leaf. The plain muslin (calico) is held with café clips decorated with seashells and raffia.

Curtain Trimmings

Interesting curtain accessories add a fillip, a special touch, to any decorative scheme. Poles, finials, rings, and other hanging devices are available in all sorts of materials, most commonly wood, metal, and plastic. Some are cheap and cheerful, some wildly expensive. Proprietary accessories are usually convenient to fit, but many unlikely things could be used or modified to reflect the theme or function of a room, or the nature of its occupants; hockey stick curtain poles, fake fruit finials, nautically knotted rope tiebacks. With a little imagination, you can dream up a whole range of exciting and completely unique effects.

ABOVE: *Light filters warmly through this linen curtain bordered with carefully frayed burlap (hessian). Tassels of button-trimmed garden raffia dangle from the hem.*

ABOVE: *A dainty treatment for a light sunny room; the pale sweep of curtain is held by a puff-ball tieback encrusted with pearl buttons.*

LEFT: *With tartan ribbons about their necks, jaunty little Scottie dogs, cut using pinking shears from double layers of check, and then stitched together, march along the hem of this bow-strewn curtain.*

Cushions

Nothing makes a chair or sofa look more inviting than a heap of plump cushions; there can never be too many. The choice of style is enormous: tailored and piped, fringed, braided and tasseled, buttoned or tied, in matching or contrasting fabrics. Whatever shape or size, whether plain or fancy, cushions make seating complete, and can look smart and sophisticated as well as luxuriously comfortable.

LEFT: *Restrained color and simple patterns, in mixed natural fabrics, combine in a rich variety of shapes and trimmings for a show of subtle sophistication.*

RIGHT: *Simple elegance for a classic wooden chair; cushions of ivory-white silk and soft wool plaid in forest tones.*

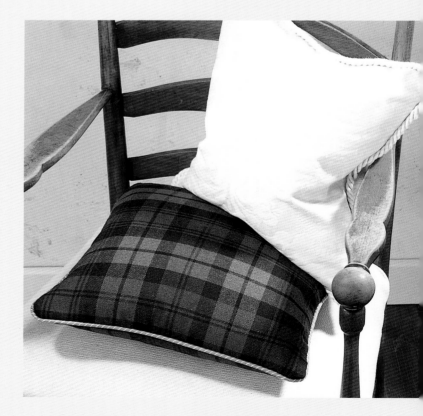

Buttoned Cushions

Buttons can be used in many imaginative ways to fasten and decorate cushion covers. They are made in an extraordinary range of materials, from hand-carved wood to glass or metal. They are easier to sew than zippers, making a feature of a fastening rather than trying to hide it.

Covers can be made to button in a variety of ways; along the edges, across the front or back of the cover, with envelope flaps or tabs, fastened with buttonholes or with loops made of fabric or cord. The cover fabric and the style of the room will dictate the choice.

OPPOSITE TOP: *Fresh blue and white checked cotton makes a cheerful, contemporary-looking cushion cover, fastened at the side with no-nonsense wooden buttons.*

OPPOSITE BOTTOM: *A collection of busy, printed covers, each made individual by a particular feature, including one with a border of large pearl buttons.*

RIGHT: *Covered buttons are used as a design feature on this classy cushion cover, punctuating the dual nature of the color combination.*

Making Buttoned Cushions

Rather than hiding an opening and fastenings, you can use it to make a striking display with contrasting or complementing buttons. Here the opening is made on the front, half of which overlaps a contrasting panel. Buttonholes are made near the overlapping edge, and buttons are sewn onto the underlapping layer.

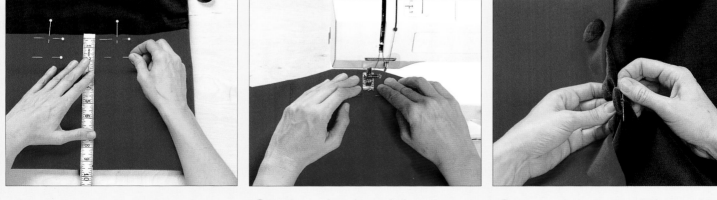

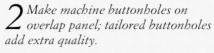

1 *Using a button as a guide, mark buttonhole positions on overlap with pins.*

2 *Make machine buttonholes on overlap panel; tailored buttonholes add extra quality.*

3 *Position buttons on underlap panel directly beneath buttonholes; sew on by hand.*

ABOVE: *A harmonious arrangement of fabrics and trimmings, with varied textures but colors in common.*

LEFT: *Contrasting silk cord sewn around the dark tartan cover links it visually with the thick rope edging of the ivory-white silk cushion.*

BELOW: *Elegant plain cushions given a sharp edge with cords of decreasing thickness; and a fabric-bordered cushion enlivened with silken key tassels.*

Trimmed Cushions

Cushions can be transformed by the addition of attractive trimmings. Piped edgings, frills, and wide fabric borders must be sewn into the seams of the cover as it is made; most cords and braids are sewn around the cover after it is completed, with tassels added at the same time.

Materials for trimmings may be chosen to contrast with the cover fabric. Cushions can be artfully arranged, with fabrics and edgings in color-coordinated groups, or so tassels and cords drape spectacularly over the furniture beneath.

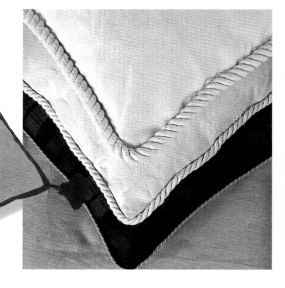

LEFT: Multicolored felt "feathers," cut out with pinking shears, have been sewn into the seam of this brilliant parrot cushion cover.

Adding a Cord Trim

Easy to apply, there are multitudes of cords available. Choose something which either picks out some colors from the cover fabric, contrasts, or matches exactly. Buy enough to go around all edges of the cushion, plus four matching tassels. Make up the cover, leaving ¾ in (2cm) open at one corner.

1 Push end of cord into opening in seam; using strong sewing thread, slipstitch cord to edge.

2 At corner, wind tassel loop around cord; continue slipstitching cord to cover.

3 At last corner apply tassel to cord; tuck end of cord into seam opening; stitch firmly in place.

159

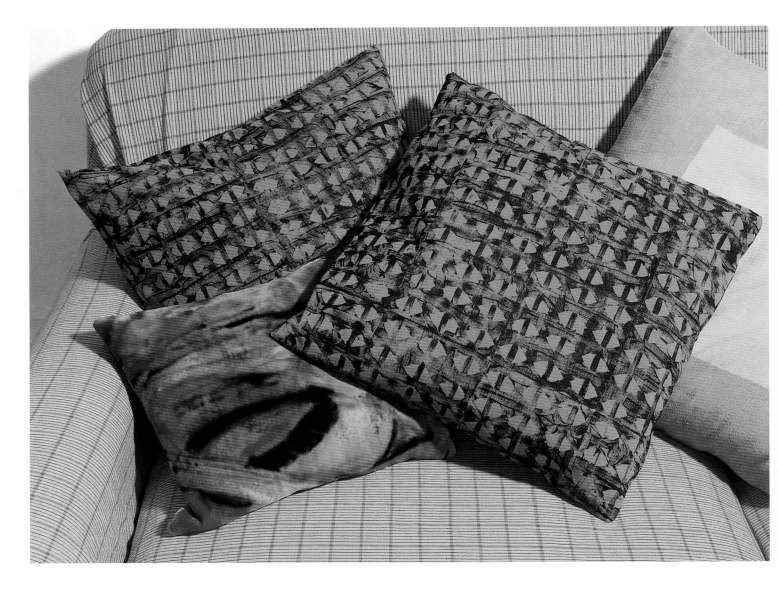

Design Variety

Like anything in a decorative scheme, cushions need to be considered as an integral part of the overall design. Each component of the design has its role, and it is often the smaller, more moveable items, like cushions, which make or break a scheme. Harmonious groupings are emphasized by a touch of contrast; equally, groups of disparate things can be united by one common element, such as color, texture, or shape.

Cushions look wonderful piled up casually, in a riot of pattern and color, with fabrics chosen to match the rest of the room and echo texture and form.

ABOVE: Cushions, covers, and colors in unity, the patterns are regular, abstract, and hand-printed.

OPPOSITE: A basketweave glassholder and chair seat, echoed in checkered ribbons woven into an exquisite cushion.

LEFT: Different shaped cushions made in plain and patterned fabrics look good together when colors are well matched.

Design ideas can be based on absolutely anything; shared colorings, shapes, or textures make easily definable themes, linking the different components of a decorative scheme.

It can be fun to use aspects of familiar objects in an unusual way. For example letter shapes could make cushions; ribbon bows for tying hair could be used to fasten covers; stuffed fabric versions of household objects, perhaps a toaster or a teapot, could put a novel slant on soft furnishings.

OPPOSITE: Crisp striped pillow ticking makes two cushion parcels; four-pointed wrappers fold up around plump, butter-yellow cushions, tied with soft bows; a simple twist for a fresh, pretty effect.

LEFT: This sweetheart cushion is tucked into a shaped, overlapped cover, and tied with a matching ribbon bow.

Tied Fastenings

Ribbons, cords, and all sorts of ready-mades may be used for ties, or they can be made of fabric to match or contrast with the cushion fabric. Make rouleau ties which are narrow and round-sectioned or flat ties for a more tailored look. Both are made from bias-cut strips and sewn onto the cover just as the ribbons are in this technique.

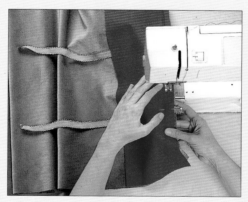

1 On opening side, pin equally-spaced ribbons between cover and flap; machine 5/8 in (1.5cm) seam including ribbons.

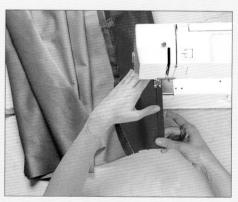

2 Open flap away from cover fabric and ribbons; machine double 1/2 in (1cm) hem on raw edge.

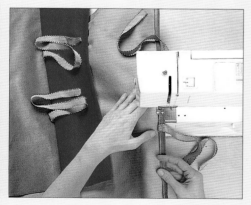

3 On cover raw edge, machine double 1/2 in (1cm) hem over tucked and refolded, equally spaced ribbons.

4 Face upward, fold hemmed edge to panel seam; fold panel over main fabric; machine side seams.

5 Turn cover right side out; insert pad; tuck flap over pad and tie ribbons into bows.

RIGHT: *A traditional, one-piece, lace cover, embroidered with flowers.*

ABOVE: *Simple classic bolster; straight extension sewn onto end of cover, gathered and finished with tassels.*

ABOVE: *Contrast pleated frill inserted between end and extension of cover; extension neatly pleated and buttoned.*

ABOVE: *Over-long cover; ends contrast-faced inside and tied like Christmas cracker using wired ribbon.*

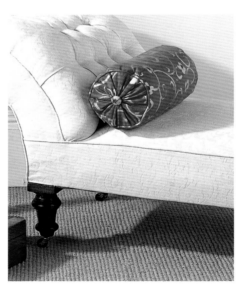

Bolsters

The good old-fashioned bolster is a versatile and attractive cushion. The simple sausage-like shape lends itself to a great variety of treatments, from easy wrap-around covers with tied ends, to some more complex constructions, finished with piping or braids and tassels.

ABOVE LEFT: *This three-piece cover has piping inserted between end and extension and a button to conceal the gathered centre.*

LEFT: *The striking fabric sewn into a tube, with ends faced inside in contrasting silk, is tied with extravagant, gold tasseled rope.*

Chair Cushions

With the addition of seat cushions, plain wooden chairs for dining or occasional use can be made to look smart and businesslike, or casually decorative to suit their surroundings. They become not only more interesting to look at, but much more comfortable to sit on.

Cushion pads may be filled with feathers or fiber, such as kapok or polyester, for a soft, informal look, or cut to the seat shape from foam for a more tailored style. Piped or frilled, cushions may be left loose, or fastened to the chair with fabric ties or tabs.

RIGHT: A plain wooden dining chair is pepped up with a bold, neatly piped, circular cushion, in contemporary checked fabric.

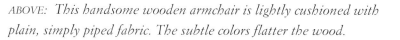

ABOVE: This handsome wooden armchair is lightly cushioned with plain, simply piped fabric. The subtle colors flatter the wood.

RIGHT: Here, another armchair is made welcoming with a frilled cover in a pretty, country floral print.

Cushions for Wicker Chairs

Comfortable cushions are almost essential for wicker chairs, whose robust woven textures might otherwise prove rather too impressive.

Wicker is a sympathetic choice for conservatory furniture and indoor-outdoor use. You can simply use scatter cushions or try well-fitted box cushions which look particularly good against the easy neutral colors of wicker and cane. Seat cushions may be slim and tailored, more like a padded cover than cushioning, or deep, squashy, and voluptuous, to sink into luxuriously.

ABOVE: A plain cover for a well-stuffed cushion; the tangerine linen with a broad, blanket-stitched border is perfect for this curvaceous chair.

RIGHT: This dignified four-square woven chair is complemented beautifully by its deep, boxy cushion, covered and neatly piped in a green and old gold classical print.

LEFT AND FAR LEFT: Two generous cushions, one with square-sided front panel and one with rollover front. Both are well-padded, rounded, and piped.

OPPOSITE: The warm gleam of wicker is set off by an inviting nest of red-and-white cushions, patchwork, lace, and cheery messages.

BELOW: *Sinuous Jacobean-style crewel-work flowers stitched in wool on linen evoke subtle antique elegance.*

Embroidered Cushions

Cushions provide an unsurpassed opportunity for showing off embroidery of every kind. From delicate, white-embroidered, fine lawn, through colorful crewel-work on linen to chunky folk-style needlepoint, there is infinite variety.

The stuffed form of a cushion ideally suits the flexible nature of embroidered fabric, the undulations of its surface highlighting the texture of the stitchery. The incorporation of beading, metallic threads, and appliqué techniques adds richness and variety to embroidered work, emphasizing and complimenting the coloring of the overall decorative scheme. As well as being absorbing and entertaining to make, embroidered cushions make wonderful gifts, with messages lovingly worked in needlepoint to commemorate special anniversaries, or as holiday souvenirs with patterns and pictures from faraway places.

OPPOSITE: *Cushions embellished with vigorous and richly textured embroidery in vibrant colors with intricate designs based on heraldic motifs.*

Simple Upholstery

While deep-buttoned upholstery looks wonderfully luxurious, it requires special skills to do, and it is not cheap. However, with straightforward techniques and lovely fabrics, simple upholstery can transform ordinary-looking furniture, with flair and perhaps a touch of intrigue, without breaking the bank.

LEFT: *This fresh check cotton cover dresses up an old wooden chair; plain cotton side panels button stylishly to the front and back.*

RIGHT: *A small side table is disguised with a crisp, full-length cover in blue and white checks, piped and tied with coordinating floral print fabric.*

Easy Fitted Covers

Where the upholstered part of an item of furniture is a separate removable piece, it is very easy to fit a new cover using only a few basic tools.

Chairs and stools can be given a complete change of identity, since, after the seat pad is removed, the chair frame can be refinished, perhaps using interesting paint techniques. The seat pad can simply be covered, new fabric being stretched over the old and tacked or stapled to the underside of its frame. The seat pad is then fitted back into the newly finished chair frame. Quick and effective, it could hardly be simpler.

ABOVE: *An old wooden chair is given a distressed paint finish in acid green and yellow, the seat covered with an uncompromisingly modern print.*

LEFT: *This stool's original woven rush seat has been replaced with similarly woven strips of gingham, its frame painted a brilliant chalky blue.*

OPPOSITE TOP: *An overstuffed stool is given star treatment with double-layered fabric. The under layer shows through the center circles of cutout star shapes, each edged with gold machine satin stitching through both layers.*

Covering a Footstool

Overstuffed upholstery (where the cushion is a raised pad, sometimes internally sprung, fixed onto a frame or legs) is also easy to cover. The seat is removed from its frame or legs; new fabric is stretched over the pad, then stapled or tacked underneath.

1 Place the padded seat on the fabric, both right side down; pin and staple stretched fabric to frame.

2 At the corners, fold the fabric neatly to form a miter; either staple or tack firmly in place.

LEFT: *Aquamarine terry towelling, with a contrast-bound wavy hem, makes a deliciously soft, comforting cover, suitably marine, for a bentwood chair in a bathroom.*

BELOW: *Simple sewn fabric ties, used here to attach a loose cover to the chair leg, provide added decorative interest.*

Slipcovers

For the price of some lovely fabric and a little effort, simple slipcovers can ring the changes and add a touch of individuality to a room. Effective disguises for battered old wooden chairs can be easily and inexpensively made. All that is required is inspiration and some basic machine-sewing skills to achieve impressive results. It is important to choose the right fabric for the room. Plain canvas or linen would make a smart cover for an old desk chair in a home office or a complete set of chairs for the dining room; a wipe-clean vinyl-coated cotton or colorful fake-fur fabric would be fun in a child's playroom. Alternatively, you could go for a more luxurious look and use thick, soft chenille to transform a director's chair that has seen better days into a supplementary armchair, not forgetting the added benefit of cutting down drafts around its back.

LEFT: *A pretty disguise for an old director's chair; floral prints in coordinated colors convert a plain folding seat into a modest but inviting easy chair.*

Making a Chair Slipcover

Simple covers can be made for all sorts of chairs. Here, three fabric panels are cut; two for the sides and one to cover from floor level in front, over seat and back, and down to the floor again. The main piece is sewn to the side panels at seat and front edges and tied with ribbons down each side of the chair back.

1 Cut paper patterns; two side pieces, one piece for front from floor over seat and back, and down to floor; allow ⅝in (1.5cm) all around.

2 Cut out fabric panels and, with wrong side out, sew side to seat and front edges; neaten remaining raw edges with ⅝in (1.5cm) hem; press seams open.

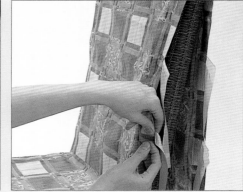

3 Fit cover on chair, right side out; stitch equally spaced pairs of ribbons all down open side edge of back; tie into bows, trimming ends.

Directors' Chairs

Apart from all the great movies made there, Hollywood is also responsible for the fame of one of the truly great chairs of all time, the director's chair. A design classic, it is light, portable, and remarkably comfortable. The seat and back are easily replaced, often without any need for sewing. Instead the fabric is nailed to the frame, and offers tremendous scope for decoration.

Rich fabrics in furnishing weights, such as velvet or satin, damask, chintz, or brocade would be suitable, if unusual; the most frequent choice is canvas, in natural or synthetic materials. Available in a vast range of colors and patterns (mostly stripes), it is a strong fabric, ideal for painting on or printing. Stenciled patterns (not forgetting type – all those directors' names) are particularly successful. Additionally, the chair can be much enhanced by painting its wooden frame to complement the canvas.

RIGHT: Lightweight and easily folded, directors' chairs are perfect for the garden. A striking stenciled pattern decorates the canvas of these two chairs, their frames painted in a contrasting soft blue-green.

ABOVE: Turquoise canvas, printed with a trellis pattern of sunflowers and sunburst motifs, makes a bright covering for a chair in a conservatory.

ABOVE: A simple geometric design, taken from the pattern on a colorful woven rug, is stamped in red on plain white canvas.

LEFT: *Crisp stripes in navy and white, piped and tied with scarlet; these neat, simple, and dramatic modern cushions combine well on an antique oak settle.*

OPPOSITE: *A deep, buttoned box cushion, covered and piped in rich woven fabric, is strewn luxuriously with cushions in a star-spangled secret alcove.*

Box Cushions

Tailored box cushions are the simplest kind of what could be called "real" upholstery, and the addition of a little neatly made piping creates an impression of the highest quality.

Box cushions are usually made to measure for specific pieces of furniture, or to fit exactly into alcove or window seats. Originally they were stuffed with horse hair, wool, or kapok. However, today modern materials are more readily available. They can be easily cut to size and make very comfortable cushions. High-density foam is excellent for a firm but resilient cushion; softer foams make cushions of similar appearance, but are more yielding.

Made with panel sides and usually piped for added crispness around the edges, box cushions may be plain, or buttoned, or tufted like a mattress. If the cover needs to be removable, a feature can be made of fabric ties, or you can insert a zipper, concealing it within one of the piped seams.

Coordinating Upholstery

To make a really strong statement in decorating a room, all elements of the treatment need to be coordinated in one way or another. The balance of hard against soft, cool against warm, is important. From floor to ceiling, window to hearth, a scheme is most successful when everything harmonizes, or when there is a sympathy between its various components.

By using upholstery fabrics in pale tones of a limited number of colors, a relaxed but strong theme is established. Different styles and textures of upholstery, fitted and slipcovers, piped and embroidered cushions, are united by the continuity of color. Subtle color changes in the same tonal range add interest without being overpowering; cushions in different colors look wonderful placed casually on the furniture, with other accessories in the same key colors adding subtle accents.

RIGHT: White and ice-cream colors in pale tones link the different elements in this beautiful airy room. Light filters through elegant panel blinds bordered with pale lime green; upholstery and cushion covers in strawberry pink, ice blue, lime, yellow, and white are softened by the subtle contrast of white-painted brick walls.

Bed Linen

Soft, down-filled duvets, lace-trimmed pillows, candy-striped cotton sheets covered with patchwork quilts – bed linen in all its glorious diversity sets the style of a bedroom.

Often the bed is the largest item of furniture in the room, providing the opportunity for a truly grand statement. Plain and functional, prettily sophisticated, or extravagantly opulent, there is scope for every different style.

LEFT: *Elegant treatment of serene simplicity; a modern four-poster, curtained, skirted, and draped with clouds of white, is adorned with a lovingly worked blue striped quilt.*

RIGHT: *Unparalleled luxury; sheets and pillowcases in fine crisp linen, embroidered and bordered with drawn-thread work and crocheted lace; classic bedclothes for a traditional bedroom.*

City Sophisticated

Restrained neutral colors and natural textures combine to create an oasis of sophisticated calm in the bustle of city life. Stone and beige used with white and cream, in subtly varied combinations of fabrics, make bed linen that is functional and unfussy, yet soothing and inviting. Color is used sparingly, in uninterrupted blocks for maximum impact, allowing the smooth drape of plain bed linen its role as focal point. Fabrics with different textures, or nearly invisible patterns, contrast or provide modest accents. An air of elegance is reinforced with tailored curtains and plain carpet, and with discreet accessories.

ABOVE: *Muted city pinstripes and checks, rough linens, slubbed raw silks, canvas; natural fabrics in colors of bleached wood, stone, and oatmeal.*

LEFT: *Perfectly plain and simple: white cotton percale sheets and soft white cotton blanket, set against off-white canvas tied over unbleached muslin.*

OPPOSITE: *Square, pearl-buttoned, putty-colored cushions serve as a restrained contrast with the pale bedspread, reflecting the two-tone bed skirt and matching bedside tablecloths.*

185

OPPOSITE: A traditional "Flying Geese" pattern is sewn in airy blue and white cottons, trimmed with scarlet.

LEFT AND BELOW: Large pieces of brushed cottons in varied checks make a bold patchwork cover; a neatly buttoned flap keeps the duvet in place.

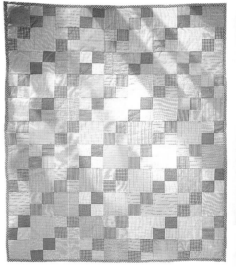

ABOVE: Stripes and checks from well-loved shirts, carefully arranged for a softly faded counterpane.

Patchwork Covers and Quilts

One of the great needlework traditions, patchwork makes the most wonderful bed covering; the unique character of any patchwork object can add the perfect finishing touch to a bedroom. Traditional patchwork patterns are many and varied, each with its own history. Some look very complicated to make, but even the most intricate designs are made simply by carefully sewing together shaped pieces of fabric, albeit many dozens or even hundreds of them. Making patchwork fabric is simpler if larger pieces of fabric are joined.

For a folk-style theme with plenty of impact, patchwork can be made into quilted counterpanes in the traditional manner, or covers for pillows and duvets, linking the colors with the room's decor. It looks best if a limited color scheme is chosen, but lots of differently patterned or textured fabrics help to give that real patchwork look.

RIGHT: A new family heirloom; baby's initials and cutout hearts, framed with gingham, make a snug sweetheart cover, the colors just right in an antique cot.

OPPOSITE: "Windmills and Hourglasses" are thickly padded in this traditional quilt in red, white, and blue.

While geometric and abstract patterns are probably the most widely used for patchwork, letters and pictorial shapes are also very effective in a design. Symbols can be cut out and sewn into panels to be arranged in a formal framework.

Patchwork is the favorite fabric for quilts, those most comforting of bedcovers. A quilt is a padded cover: batting (wadding) is sandwiched between two layers of fabric, and stitched through all the layers to hold them together. The stitching may follow a regular checkerboard grid or other pattern, or be tufted like a mattress, or simply follow the main pattern shapes of the patchwork.

LEFT: Checkerboard-quilted oriental prints, backed with a hand-painted ideogram and bordered with stripes.

A Lacy Look

For simple elegance and prettiness, lace is hard to beat. A bed covered with heavy, handmade lace, piled high with soft, white, lace-trimmed pillows, is romantic and inviting like no other.

Lace is made in countless patterns and qualities, from gossamer nets to rich, crocheted florals. A set of plain bed linen can be made luxurious with the addition of frilled hems of eyelet (broderie anglaise), or a wide band of antique lace stitched across a pillowcase. Other needlecraft techniques – embroidery, drawn thread work, appliqué, and quilting – all combine beautifully with lace, particularly when executed in white on white to match the linen. Lacy fabrics look particularly effective when laid over other different colored fabrics, or when given a lift with a little colored embroidery or ribbon, the contrast emphasizing the country-fresh delicacy of the lace. Intrinsically pretty, lace nevertheless makes a strong visual statement, simultaneously suggesting femininity and grace while giving a hint of sensuous extravagance.

ABOVE: *A lavish collection of plump pillows and cushions, lace and embroidery, has dashes of colorful cross stitch and ribbons.*

OPPOSITE: *White-on-white embroidery, lace, linen, and net, offer a delicate contrast for mellow country furniture.*

Floral Bedcovers

Flowers, realistic or stylized, are the most popular decorative motifs in all soft furnishings; they are colorful and grow in a variety of distinctive, strong shapes which lend themselves perfectly to fabric design.

The lightness and fragility of flowers are beautifully expressed with embroidery, and fine strong fabrics, like silk and linen, are excellent for intricately stitched work. Printed or woven floral patterns are equally attractive, and can be embellished with braids or fringed borders. Styles of design, and thus, naturally, of pattern for print and embroidery, alter with fashion and the age. A room decorated in keeping with a specific historical period needs to be furnished and upholstered with an appreciation of the styles of the time. Genuinely contemporary bedcovers, if they can be found, give integrity to period decorative schemes for bedrooms, supplemented by other soft furnishings in sympathetic colors and materials.

RIGHT: A magnificent carved oak four-poster, complete with poem-emblazoned tester matches an exquisite embroidered bedcover with roses, poppies, and hawthorn crowded into a treasure of love knots.

LEFT: *This pretty, stylized floral print has a fresh rural charm, suiting the light airiness of the room. Printed flower stems echo the sweeping iron curves of the Victorian bedstead.*

Attaching Fringing

Decorative fringes add interest and glamor to a bedcover and also have the benefit of extra weight at the hem to improve the drape. For a reversible cover, a fringe trimming can be attached so that it is seen on only one side of the cover; on the other side the trimming is hidden under the cover's hem.

1 Using double-sided fabric, pin fringe to edges, with fringe trimming slightly overlapping fabric edge; stitch along fabric edge of trimming.

2 Turn fringe back to other side of fabric, covering raw edge; pin in place. Turn corners with particular care, basting if necessary.

3 Machine-stitch fringe trimming to fabric along top edge. Both sides of cover may be used, either showing or concealing top of fringe trimming.

Directory

It is useful to have an idea of the range of materials available for making soft furnishings in order to make a good choice when planning a project. On the following pages a selection of fabrics and fillings, finials and fittings is shown as a guide when selecting materials. This Directory acts as a starting point for exploring the wide world of soft furnishings.

LEFT: *A small selection of materials from the soft furnishings treasury; silks, threads, buttons, linens, scissors, thimble, tape-measure; good quality aids good results.*

RIGHT: *Time put aside for accurate measuring and marking is time well spent; it can be expensive to recut. Rulers, pencils, and tailor's chalk are essential.*

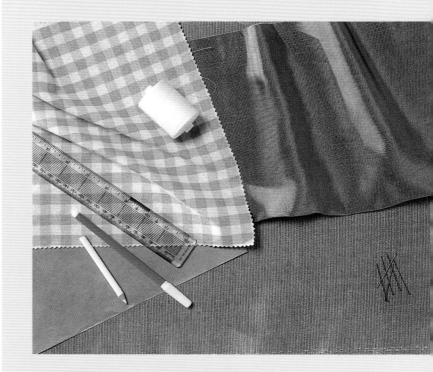

Fabric Glossary

Quite apart from their differences in color and pattern, fabrics are made for many different specific uses, and in a huge variety of textures. The samples here show just a tiny selection, in themed groups: constructional fabrics used for the basics of soft furnishings; printed patterned fabrics; some rich, luxurious pile fabrics; neutral colored fabrics in different weaves and fibers; woven checked fabrics; woven figured fabrics; fabrics with a variety of textural interest.

While fabrics are usually designed for a particular purpose, with a little inventiveness, most can be used in more than one way. It can be interesting to mix textiles of different qualities for contrast and impact. Recognition of the similarities, as well as the differences between fabrics – color, texture, weave – helps when choosing a coordinated scheme.

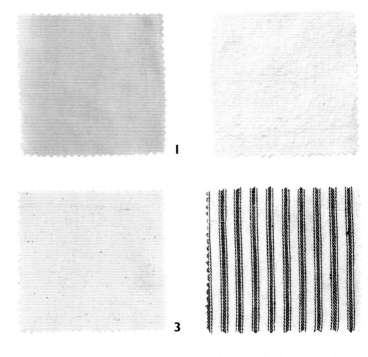

1 Plain cotton curtain lining. 2 Interlining: thick cotton, for curtain insulation and body. 3 Unbleached muslin (calico): firm, tough, used for close upholstery. 4 Black-striped ticking: cushions, upholstery.

5 Printed cotton: infinitely varied. 6 Printed linen: strong, even, excellent for slipcovers and curtains. 7 Cotton chintz: detailed prints, sometimes glazed. 8 Paisley: traditional printed wool or cotton.

9 Printed velvet: rich dramatic pile fabric. 10 Silk damask: woven raised pattern, flat background, silk sheen. 11 Chenille damask: soft, fluffy pile, raised pattern. 12 Striped velvet: raised pile stripes.

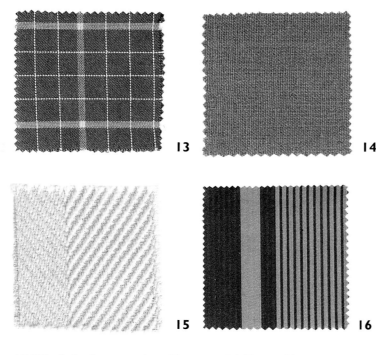

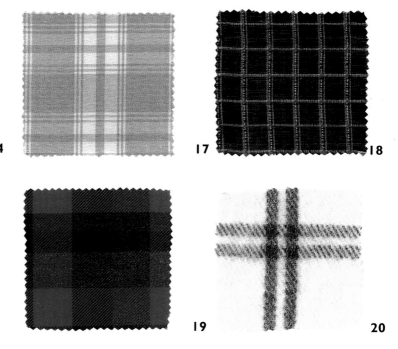

13 *Wool checks: smooth twill weave.* 14 *Natural linen: strong, even, drapes beautifully; upholstery and curtains.*
15 *Herringbone cotton: bold weave, hardwearing, thick; curtains.* 16 *French ticking: closely woven; upholstery.*

17 *Cotton check; sturdy, versatile.* 18 *Checked silk: luxurious, lustrous colors, slub-inlaid woven grid.* 19 *Wool tartan: even, colorful, warm; drapes beautifully.* 20 *Soft blanket: loose weave, cozy.*

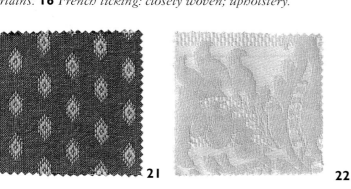

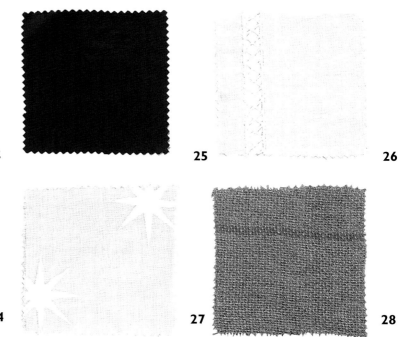

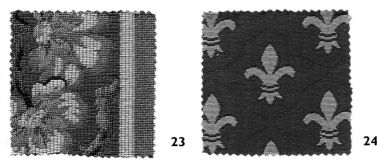

21 *Cotton and linen mix: blinds, upholstery.* 22 *Wool damask: soft, heavy; excellent for curtains, insulator.* 23 *Tapestry: rich patterns, heavy, textured; curtains, covers.* 24 *Heavy cotton weave: double-sided.*

25 *Silk taffeta: brilliant, two-tone.* 26 *Cotton with open grid: sheer cotton, grid adds lightness.* 27 *Printed lightweight muslin: fine, translucent, print adds texture.* 28 *Burlap (hessian): rough, tough, characterful.*

Curtain Poles and Finials

Curtains which are to be pulled are generally hung from poles or special rods (tracks), but are also sometimes strung or wired in place. Rods (tracks) are usually hidden by the curtain heading, or by a cornice (pelmet) or valance, while poles are positively featured. Some traverse (corded) systems imitate the look of brass poles and rings by using ring-fronted runners, drawn with cords.

There is a vast selection of poles, rings, and brackets available, in wood, metal, and plastics, and it is not difficult to install them, nor to improvise unique and interesting poles from apparently unlikely objects. Most poles come with their own finials, which act as stoppers at either end, but you can mix and match to create your own unique look.

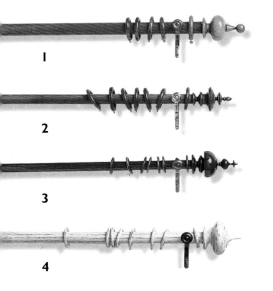

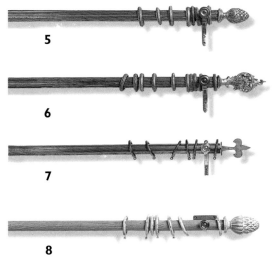

LEFT: **1** *Turned finial, wooden pole.* **2** *Antique pole and accessories; keen hunting unearths great finds.* **3** *Rich, dark polished wood.* **4** *Distressed paint for wooden pole.* **5** *Fluted brass pole, matching rings and pineapple finial.* **6** *Ornate finial for lovely old rail.* **7** *Brass fleur-de-lis finial and pole.* **8** *Solid pole and finial.*

LEFT: A brass bracket screwed to the window frame makes a handsome support for a plain wooden pole with turned finials. Curtains can be hung with the pole and rings remaining visible.

RIGHT: Poles and finials are usually matched for materials and size, though a thin rail can also look good with an oversized finial.

ABOVE: Four finials: modern chrome, traditional and ornate brass, and simple gilded wood.

RIGHT: A generous finial for a thick wooden pole, turned and carved, and given a worn gold finish.

ABOVE: 1 Unpainted plain wooden pole. 2 Plastic rod (track) with slide-in runners. 3 Metal rod (track) with nylon gliders. 4 Polished brass café curtain rail. 5 Expanding tension-spring rod. 6 Plastic-covered spring wire for sheers. 7 Wrought-iron rod with curly finial.

Curtain Rods (Tracks)

There is a variety of curtain rod (track) types available, designed for specific sliding runners, and for various curtain heading tapes. The rod (track) is clipped into supporting brackets screwed to the wall above the window at regular intervals. Plastic gliders are fitted on the track to take the curtain hooks.

Some tracks are finished with decorative patterns on the front face, while others are plain, and would benefit from the addition of a cornice (pelmet) or valance.

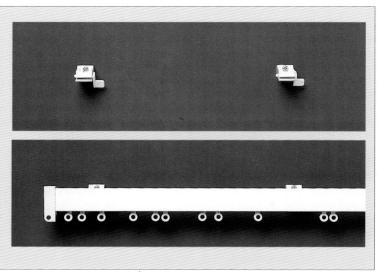

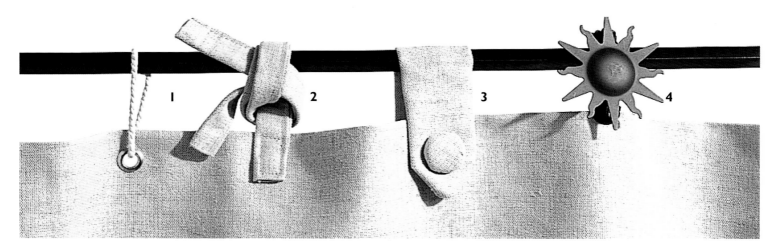

Curtain Rings and Headings

From plain sewn casings to tapes for making complex patterns of pleats, the purpose of any heading is to hold a curtain onto its hanging rail. This can be achieved in many ways, and there are dozens of inspired possibilities for that special spark of interest.

Pleating and gathering tapes for curtain headings require varying amounts of fabric width, for modest pleats or very full curtains, and for degrees of formality and extravagance. Apart from added fittings, the curtain fabric itself can be shaped to make integral "hooks," particularly where the curtain does not have to be pulled across too often.

ABOVE: Headings for stationary curtains. **1** *Cord through grommets (eyelets).* **2** *Fabric or ribbon ties sewn to curtain.* **3** *Tab with decorative button trim fastened over rod.* **4** *Café clip, sun motif adds interest.*

RIGHT: **1** *Rod pocket (slot) heading: simple sewn casing; stationary curtains.* **2** *Goblet pleats: long formal curtains, rich fabrics.* **3** *Gathered heading: versatile, suits all uses.* **4** *Box pleats: neat, elegant, used here with clips.*

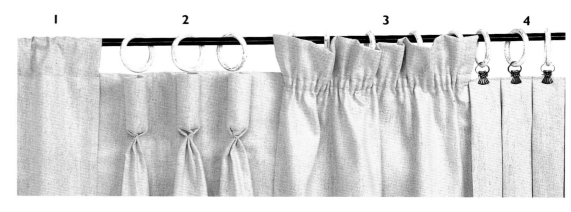

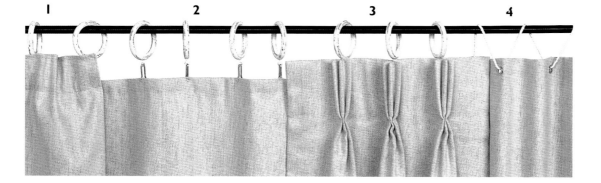

LEFT: **1** *Pencil pleats: flexible style.* **2** *Hand-sewn hooks: simple, ungathered, with hooks visible.* **3** *Pinch pleats: formal triple pleats; suits long curtains.* **4** *Grommets (eyelets): die-punched brass with cord; informal, stylish.*

ABOVE: *Hints of the East: black iron rod and rings for bold, exotic print.*

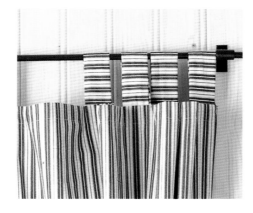

ABOVE: *Generously cut tabs in well-matched stripes slide easily on a thin rod.*

ABOVE: *Specially dyed tape stitched to front of curtain, gathered, and tied with matching ribbon bows.*

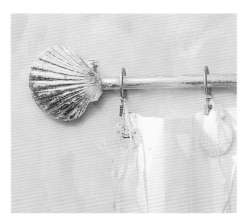

ABOVE: *Seashells and raffia, clip-ringed on a simple, gold leaf encrusted doweling pole.*

ABOVE: *Scooped and brass-ringed heading hangs café curtains on a thin brass rail; rings are sewn on.*

ABOVE: *Warm, striped double curtain, front and lining draped separately from simple sewn casing.*

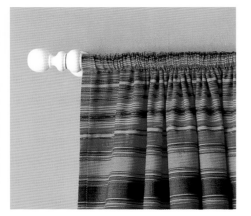

ABOVE: *Smooth pole and big enough casing ensures easy-running curtain also stays put.*

ABOVE: *Checked picket fence panels, joined, punched with grommets (eyelets), and threaded on a strong cord.*

ABOVE: *Gloriously simple: golden sunshine bracket supports gilded pole and curtain with sewn casing.*

Tiebacks and Tassels

Luxurious tiebacks, or some heavy, corded tassels, put the final touch to well-made curtains and blinds. Fittings and cord pulls for blinds and curtains are available in various styles; tassels are easily custom-made using skeins of embroidery thread or yarn, doubled and tied onto a loop, the ends trimmed evenly and shaken into shape. For tiebacks, if the curtain can be gathered into or tucked behind it, anything goes, from knotted rope to horse brasses on brackets.

ABOVE: Commercially made luxurious tiebacks; beautiful corded silk tassels, embellished with woven patterns.

LEFT: Easy-to-make tassels, using colored embroidery thread wound around card, bound and trimmed.

ABOVE: Tassels and bicolored cords, supple, gleaming silk.

Traditional Tiebacks

ABOVE: Braided jute ropes, elegant, sophisticated.

ABOVE: Classic, silk and cotton, heavily tasseled.

ABOVE: Dramatic double tassel, striking two-tone look.

ABOVE: Robust natural-fiber tassel with heavy crown.

Alternative Tiebacks

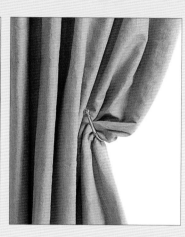
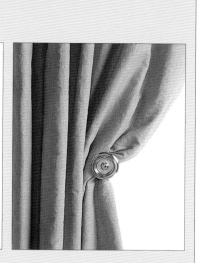

ABOVE: *A band of tapestry gathers this drape.*

ABOVE: *Slender brass hook, screwed to wall.*

ABOVE: *Silk cord, casually twisted, tied around curtain.*

ABOVE: *Elegant plain brass rosette wall bracket holdback.*

Pull cords for blinds.

Securing hooks for blinds.

RIGHT: **1** *Plain, luxuriously heavy corded silk tassels.* **2** *Woven crowns and broad braided bands.* **3** *Light and pretty multiple tassels, cheerfully corded.* **4** *A single red tassel, elegantly emphatic.*

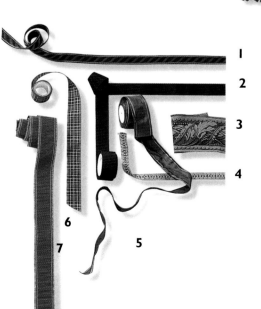

LEFT: *Materials for alternative tiebacks.* **1** *Grosgrain (petersham); all widths, lustrous.* **2** *Rich black velvet, for classic emphasis.* **3** *Wide tapestry banding; rich, traditional.* **4** *Gimp; woven and braided trimming.* **5** *"Posable" silk ribbon edged with wire.* **6** *Brightly colored woven silk tartan ribbon.* **7** *Contrast-bordered ribbon in fine grosgrain (petersham) weave.*

221

Pads and Fillings

The type of cushion required dictates the choice of filling. Fire-retardant polyurethane foam, cut to size, gives a square-sided, tailored look, sometimes softened with synthetic batting (wadding). Down and feather fillings make luxurious cushions, which compress easily but can be plumped back to size. Cushion pads should be made a little large for their covers, for a cozy, well-filled look.

ABOVE: Foam chips: cheap, tend to lumpiness, good for floor and outdoor use.

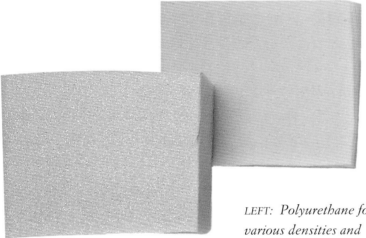

LEFT: Polyurethane foam: various densities and thicknesses, cut to size.

ABOVE: Polystyrene beads: ideal for beanbag, need cotton drill liner bag.

LEFT: Polyester batting (wadding): range of thicknesses and widths.

ABOVE: Polyester filling resilient, washable modern version of kapc

222

ABOVE: *Domette and bump: thick, woven, soft cotton; quilting natural fabrics.*

RIGHT: *Pure goose down: ultimate best choice for cushions and duvets, lasts for years.*

ABOVE: *Cotton fillings: mattresses and futons; tend to compress and become hard in time.*

RIGHT: *Down and feather: the more down there is than feather the better; cushions, quilts.*

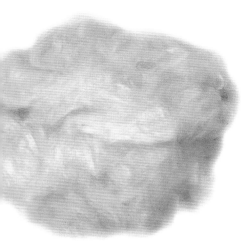

Kapok: soft natural fiber for ...ns, will eventually become lumpy.

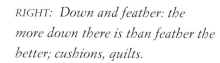

RIGHT: *Feather: cheapest feather filling, loses resilience.*

DECORATING WITH PAINT AND PAPER

Introduction

Whether painting, or covering with paper, fabric, ceramics, or wood, surface treatments can completely transform a room. Carefully harmonized and subtly textured colors make a sympathetic setting for richly decorated furniture; plain wooden floors can be patterned and patinated to suggest elegance and grandeur; whole fantasy worlds can be created with brush and paint.

LEFT: *Painted walls complement painted wooden banisters and differing textures on floor and stairs in this hallway, a complex space to decorate.*

RIGHT: *A simple, elegant treatment: a wall is dragged in two tones of yellow, with a chair rail to break the effect.*

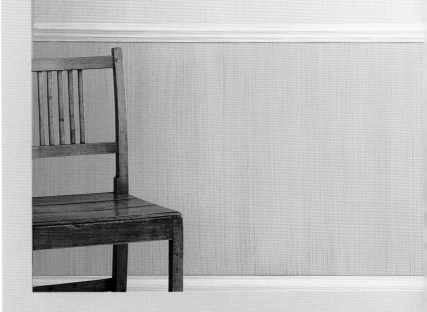

Paint Techniques

A great range of decorative painting techniques has been developed over the years, both to vary flat surface treatments, and to imitate other materials such as stone and wood. Most of these textural techniques use glazes, or coats of thinned paint, in single or multiple layers over an opaque base to achieve their effect. A glaze is a transparent medium, colored with paint or pigment, which dries slowly and so can be manipulated. Any surface can be treated, although a smooth ground will show off the texture of the finish to the greatest advantage.

Glazes may be oil-based or water-based, and while the traditional ingredients make wonderful authentic glazes

Ragging. Wet glaze is dabbed off with a loosely crumpled cotton rag to reveal the underlying color; close-toned colors look delicate, subtle.

Marbling. Sponging and ragging are combined with carefully colored glazes, overlaid and brush-softened to imitate real marble.

Rag rolling. Here a sausage-shape of cotton rag is rolled upward over wet glaze, removing it irregularly; repeated glazes are laid and rolled.

Colorwashing. Soft, natural looking; slightly darker glaze is applied over a light base and wiped gently with a soft cloth, removing brush marks.

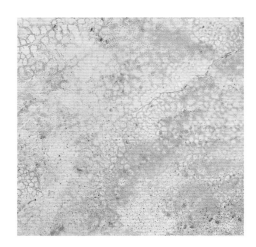

Patterning with cloth. A small, rounded pad of fine cotton fabric is dabbed over wet glaze, removing it unevenly, for a cloudy effect.

Sponging. Quick and easy; with natural or synthetic sponge, colored glaze is applied over a basecoat, or lifted off to reveal the color underneath.

and colors, proprietary modern water-based versions that are made using synthetic materials are now widely available.

The effects produced by paint techniques which use overlaid glazes and thinned washes of color with specialty brushes or simple rags and sponges, can be very subtle and natural-looking, particularly those that imitate real materials. They can also be more obviously contrived, with strongly contrasting colors that on purpose create a dramatic emphasis.

It is not difficult to achieve spectacular and truly unique effects with these painting techniques, and, reassuringly, if the results are not quite satisfactory at first, it is easy to wipe off a wet glaze and start again.

Stippling. A sophisticated finish, at first glance untextured; glaze is removed using a special, densely bristled brush, creating a subtle, even texture.

Frottage. This technique does not use glaze; thinned paint is applied then removed unevenly by pressing newspaper or fabric onto the wet layer.

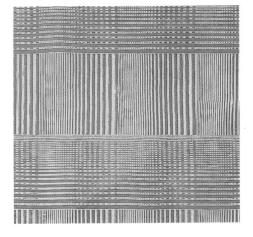

Combing. Using a special tool, the top color is combed through to reveal color underneath; further layers can be added for check effects.

Woodgraining. Like marbling, an imitation of the real thing; combed, stippled, and brushed glazes are combined for realistic effects.

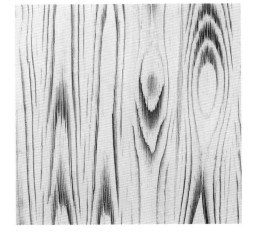

Decorative graining. A more intentionally artificial effect, which uses a special tool to make various patterns, from knotty pine to watered silk.

Dragging. A long-bristled brush is used to make smooth stripes in the glaze, for a variegated effect; stripes are clearer if contrasting colors are used.

LEFT: *Combed walls, stenciled with oriental motifs make a rich backdrop for colorful treasures.*

OPPOSITE: *Rich decoupage decoration is beautifully complemented by velvety, terra-cotta stippled walls.*

ABOVE: *Subtle, roughly colored walls with a cutout frieze of leaves make a perfect foil for glistening seashells, smooth marble, and pine.*

Decorating Options

Paint and paper are the two most basic decorating materials, but each has boundless possibilities and endless variety. For immediate effect and complete flexibility, paint is an obvious choice. Simple changes of color radically alter the look of a room, from cool, dark serenity to rich, lively warmth. Its varied qualities of luster, transparency or opacity, and texture mean that paint is the single most versatile means of decorating. Papered surfaces are readily painted, the texture of the paper adding to the richness of the paint coating.

Painted effects bring interest and focus to a wall treatment; all-over patterns and textures can be embellished with stenciled or freely painted motifs for added impact; cutout paper motifs, repeated or combined, or single images, make a picture gallery, becoming part of the wall itself.

RIGHT: Swagged gold stenciled on soft dark green walls links the tortoiseshell frame and the verdigris and gold decorated treasures on the table.

ABOVE: A collection of woodgrained objects is enhanced by blue stained matchboarding, color singing out from behind the warm wood tones.

OPPOSITE: The curving S-shapes from this steel and cane shelving unit are echoed in the stamped, stenciled, and painted decoration on walls and crockery.

Paint can be used to transform furnishings of all sorts, not only concealing and disguising the underlying characteristics of the surfaces on which it is used, but also exaggerating and enhancing their qualities. Dense flat paint absorbs light and gives a feeling of warmth; high gloss paint seems harder, cooler, more formal. Translucent or transparent paints highlight texture, particularly when used on wood – they allow the grain to show through in all its glory.

By varying the surface quality with texture or pattern applied to the whole area, a large wall or piece of furniture can be made to seem smaller, less bare, while still allowing for the display of objects both on and near it. Similarly, a well-chosen motif, painted or applied to a plain color, in gold or another contrasting color, focuses attention on particular features, perhaps framing or underlining a specific detail.

The Complete Look

A major element in a successful decorative scheme is a sense of coherence. Most rooms contain many disparate elements, such as furniture, books, ornaments, and temporary decorations such as plants or flowers, all of which contribute to the feel of the room. Decor which strives to unite all these things in a pleasing whole achieves a stimulating, and deeply satisfying, complete look.

Harmonious color, linking fixed furnishings with more movable items, makes a solid foundation for the overall scheme. Components can be matched or contrasted, breaking up large areas of plain color with interest supplied by different patterns or textures, furnishings or ornaments, chosen to complement the underlying themes of the decor. Accessories add the living character to a room, making points of focus and activity which often define its function. Their shape, color, and texture make dramatic accents to underline and emphasize the style of the decoration, while the careful use of contrast brings a touch of energy to the look.

OPPOSITE: Marbled panels, grained chair rail, and plaster-effect walls, executed in warm Mediterranean colors, make a serene backdrop for light wicker and cane furniture in a summery garden room.

BELOW: Subtle textural variety is emphasized by stark, contrast-colored dishes, with ragged paint above, and colorwashing below the plate rail painted in similarly toned gray.

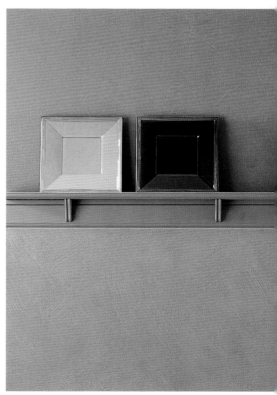

LEFT: Antique mahogany stands elegantly against the irregular frottaged pattern of soft yellow walls, and deeper yellow sponging below the chair rail.

Painted Walls

Walls offer large expanses for creative treatment. Paint can revitalize an old battered surface, and it can be used to simulate different materials. Patterned and layered, smoothed, distressed, or used pictorially, paint is a versatile decorative finish, with unlimited possibilities. As colored backgrounds for main furnishings, walls can be textured with subtle or bold paint effects, or can act as grand canvases for illusory paintings.

LEFT: This ocean view is not what it seems; stunning trompe l'oeil painting, framed with painted wooden cladding, transforms a blank wall in a conservatory.

RIGHT: Butter yellow paint, colorwashed onto soft plaster walls, brings sunshine into a bathroom fresh with bright blue glass and towels; a sympathetic, colorful treatment.

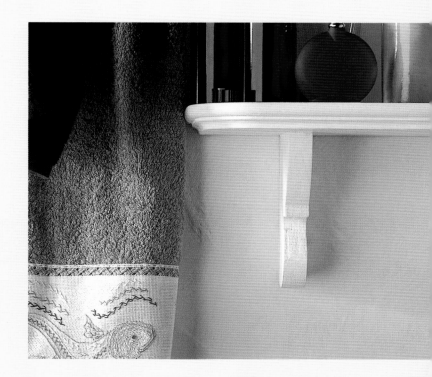

Bright and Bold

Color makes a strong impact, probably the first impression to register in any room; the decor is given vitality and flair by combinations of rich, saturated colors.

A brightly colored decorative scheme allows for dramatic use of contrast, both in color and scale; bold statements made with painted woodwork and furniture set a mood of exuberance and fun. The use of complementary colors, those opposite each other in the spectrum, enhances the strength of color. Appropriate neutrals, particularly black and white, provide accents for emphasis. Overall color statements are reinforced by the use of borders and friezes to frame and concentrate attention on specific areas and details.

The effect of strong color need not be overpowering; walls painted with kaleidoscopic layers of zingy colors have a vibrancy which energizes the room and its contents.

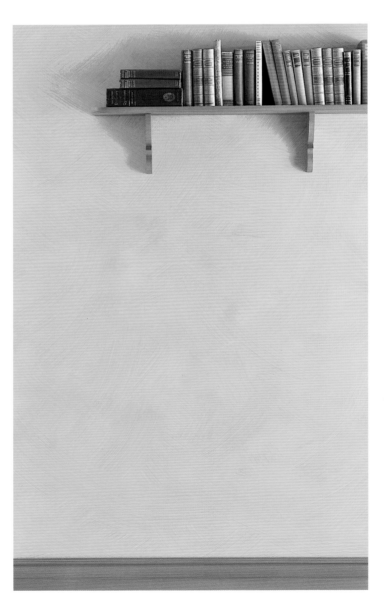

ABOVE: Delicious tomato red and mint green combine for a Mexican carnival feel.

RIGHT: Rich blue painted woodwork complements bold egg-yolk yellow walls.

OPPOSITE: Sunny ocher walls cheer and flatter solid furnishings.

238

Plain Backgrounds

Plain, simple rooms sometimes demand plain decorative treatments. Traditional paint finishes such as limewash or calcimine (distemper) have an organic quality; they soak deep into the surface of a wall, coloring the actual body of the plaster. Dry pigment can be added to the wash, giving a soft, faded tint of color, and drying to a soft, chalky luster which perfectly suits a country style or antique setting.

Paint techniques such as stippling or dragging, where the pattern created is even and not too directional, can be rendered in subtly different colors to make an apparently plain yet characterful effect.

RIGHT: A green limewash has been used to color the gentle undulations of old plaster in this country kitchen.

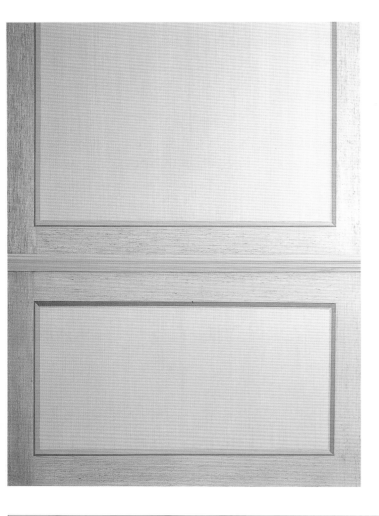

LEFT: *Subtle trompe l'oeil panels, dragged in soft colors, suggest calm sophistication.*

BELOW: *Traditional calcimine (distemper), oil-bound for durability, coats the uneven walls in this kitchen, making a perfect backdrop for the cream painted china cupboard.*

Dragging Glaze

Dragging uses a brush with long, coarse bristles to create an even, linear effect, ideal for formal treatments. The effect is subtle when worked in close-toned colors, or bold in contrasting shades. Flogging is a variation of the technique; the surface is dragged then hit, or "flogged," with the brush, breaking up the stripes.

1 Apply a thin layer of glaze in vertical strips; brush out evenly.

2 With same glaze brush, lightly smooth out glaze, making light striped pattern.

3 Hold dragging brush almost parallel to surface; draw vertically through glaze.

4 Soften effect by brushing lightly at a slight angle to the stripes.

Sponging and Ragging

Sponging and ragging are simple techniques which either remove or add layers of broken color to produce rich, sophisticated results. Colors of similar temperature and tone create an impression of depth, while a contrasting shade adds a striking and individual dimension.

Sponging is more regular on a large surface than ragging; sponge re-forms readily, so predictable patterns can be made if desired, with a variety of sponge textures from natural sea sponges for soft shapes, to sharply cut synthetic sponge. A rag can be used as a neat pad, or crumpled loosely for a soft effect, or rolled across the glaze for an expansive treatment. Cotton fabric is the usual choice for ragging, but paper towels, plastic bags, burlap (hessian), canvas, or all sorts of fabric can be used, producing very different results.

BELOW: Scattered with stenciled motifs, a warm color scheme for a bathroom uses shades of apricot for the draped chiffon swag and to sponge soft clouds over the walls.

LEFT: Pale ocher enriched with a touch of terra-cotta was ragged over an off-white ground, set against deep gray paneling for a classy effect.

Sponging Paint

Sponging can be either subtractive – where a glaze or diluted paint coat is applied to a surface and then removed while wet by dabbing off with a sponge – or additive, as shown here, where successive layers of color, glaze or dilute paint, are built up by dabbing onto the surface with a sponge.

1 Apply base color; prepare three colors for sponging, each diluted 50:50 with water.

2 Dip sponge into darkest color; dab onto wall, turning to vary marks.

3 Wash and dry sponge thoroughly; apply second color more patchily to fill gaps.

4 Repeat process with lightest color; stand back to check overall look.

Paint Effects

The basic techniques used in decorative paint finishes can be varied to create an infinite range of effects. The surface to which the paint is applied can influence the choice, as well as the outcome, of the technique. Rough plaster adds greatly to the charm of a gentle, overall wash of color, while a bland new wall can be given interest and character with a more contrived and complex patterned treatment.

There are few surfaces, even furniture and fabrics, which cannot be coated with one type of paint or another. The adventurous use of color, and different degrees of gloss or transparency, all add excitement and vitality to decorated walls, making surfaces expressive in their own right as well as providing a stimulating backdrop for other furnishings.

OPPOSITE: Vigorous, rough colorwashed walls perfectly complement robust furnishings and exotic curtain fabric.

BELOW: Feather-light sweeps of translucent green wash over walls and furniture impart an air of fresh but casual elegance.

ABOVE: Vivid, combed terra-cotta "tiles" and a dragged, steel-gray chair rail underline a wall colorwashed in thundercloud gray.

ABOVE RIGHT: Realism is not the intention here; shimmering near-complementary red and blue emphasize this dramatic, decorative woodgraining effect.

Combinations of different techniques look wonderful. Walls treated with an all-over texture can be given firm boundaries with a formal patterned effect below a chair rail. Dragging, graining, combing – all linear patterns – lend themselves to use on woodwork, creating a link with more expansively patterned walls.

Textured effects which work well on walls can be extended to doors and window frames, giving a real sense of unity to the decor. Techniques such as stippling, frottage, rag rolling, and sponging are very effective used in this way, particularly where different colors are used for the woodwork and the walls, and where the effect is applied in very carefully graded tones. Strong decorative patterns are made even more dramatic by using well-differentiated colors. Introducing a contrast makes a more dynamic impression, and mixing busy textures in coordinated tones or using high-contrast colors in well-defined patterns makes for bold decorative effects.

ABOVE: Using two quite different colors achieves a sophisticated look with frottage, here removing blue to reveal olive brown.

LEFT: Subtle frottage is used here for old, uneven walls, and is equally appropriate in aged buff tones for the woodwork.

Trompe l'Oeil

There is a long tradition of trompe l'oeil painting, both as architectural decoration and as fine art. For centuries, the idea of creating an illusion has been applied to parts of buildings, to disguise and enhance, or to make a philosophical or humorous point.

Trompe l'oeil can be used to enliven a blank wall in a room, perhaps with an artificial outside view. It can also serve to reinvent structural details: a plain wall pillar could become a Corinthian column, or wainscoting in a child's room could be transformed into a railway train. While some complex and ambitious ideas might require high levels of drawing skill, it is not difficult to achieve stunning results with the use of photocopies, tracing paper, wit, and enthusiasm; with trompe l'oeil, the idea itself is at least as important as the final result.

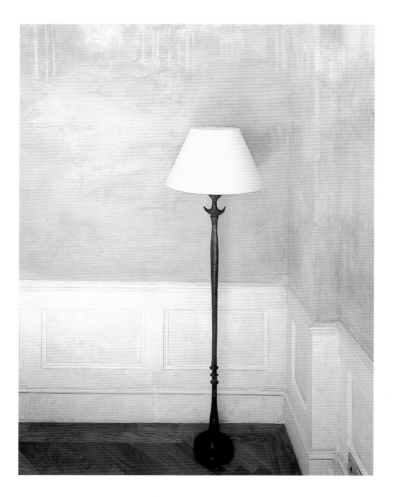

ABOVE: *This simple, graphic painting of an umbrella stand is a droll touch positioned next to a door.*

LEFT: *A light, impressionistic landscape, painted freely in fresco style, re-creates the magical atmosphere of a distant wooded glade.*

OPPOSITE: *Classical balusters transform this counter, echoing the curve of its canopy; simple, elegant shapes are rendered in cool, restrained monochrome.*

Painted Stone

Paint can be used to imitate the various kinds of stone favored for decoration. Sponging, stippling, ragging, and frottage all have their place in re-creating the colors and textures of marble, granite, and limestone, and with careful observation of examples of the real thing, all types of stone can be reproduced.

With its subtle dignity and strength, stone is well suited to formal rooms, or where an impression of space is important. It is also ideal for grand features and focal points, for example staircases or fire surrounds. The patterns and textures of natural stone are distinctive, their colors mostly muted, though some, such as malachite and some forms of marble, are vividly colored. The more formal types of stone – marble, alabaster, onyx – are most convincing when represented on smooth surfaces.

BELOW: Gray, granite-like textures have been stippled and sponged over pale ocher, carefully masked to imitate joints.

ABOVE: Classic alabaster blocks are beautifully painted here; the grain direction is thoughtfully varied and subtly colored; fine veining and precise joints produce a cool, elegant effect.

ABOVE: Delicate marbled color covers the door and paneling, making the most of a varied surface, using a very limited palette to create a worn, antique stone effect.

Stone Clad Effect

The block formation of stone cladding is easily re-created using frottaged layers of paint. Colors for representing stone are mostly neutrals, but can be tinted to coordinate with other decoration. By repeating the basic frottage process with several closely related colors, a subtle rendering of stone can be achieved; detailed joints could be drawn to add definition.

1 Apply basecoat; roughly paint lighter color in pattern of cladding.

2 Frottage wet, dilute paint with newspaper cut or torn to block shapes.

RIGHT: *Roughly cut stencils of symbols based on ancient Celtic patterns have been printed in a loosely repeating pattern with glue size, then gilded for a simple but rich effect.*

ABOVE: *Simple five-pointed stars form a constellation above the bed. Carefully positioned to avoid making a stiff, regular pattern, they are stenciled in chalky blue on a clouded yellow wall.*

Stenciling Abstract Patterns

One of the oldest forms of printing, stenciling is a versatile and exciting technique. Many civilizations have used stencils as part of their art tradition, and there is a wealth of stenciled imagery, both symbolic and figurative, for inspiration. Single abstract shapes or symbols can be stenciled in groups, or spread in orderly patterns or at random over large areas. The great charm of stenciling lies in the fact that, while a stencil can be used again and again, each

LEFT: *This striking pattern uses one stencil, a motif with four pairs of lines and four diamonds, repeated as a frieze around the room, then parts of the whole are selectively repeated to complete the design.*

print is always just slightly different from the last. Combinations of simple abstract shapes can be stenciled to build up strong compositions, or to make repeating patterns to cover large areas, rather like wallpaper. Color can be applied very evenly and densely, or it can be graded and blended. Glue size can also be printed to be flocked or gilded.

Single motifs offer flexibility of design, as the stencil can be moved about with each printing; multiple stencils are more manageable if the area to be covered is large.

ABOVE: *As an alternative to wallpaper, stenciling is inexpensive, quick to do, and very versatile; here a bold, loosely drawn trellis is roughly printed, for a lively effect.*

ABOVE: *Stenciled ribbons and roses, shaded in pink with crisp green leaves, make a frieze, matching linens, and a headboard decoration.*

Stenciling Florals

Flowers are widely used in stenciling, their shapes are easy to trace and cut out of paperboard (card), and they give great scope for imaginative combinations of color and design. Floral motifs are often used together with motifs of bows and ribbons, making swags and garlands. They are easily adapted to fit the situations where they are to be used, and can be repeated and interconnected to build up complex patterns and set compositions. Stencils representing the stylized shapes of plants can be surprisingly sophisticated for such a simple technique, and with sensitive use of color, applied with subtlety, stenciled floral decorations can look stylish and elegant, as well as very pretty.

ABOVE: *Beautifully drawn and stenciled trompe l'oeil lilies in pots are complemented by sinuous ivy, trailing above the lights and picture rail.*

LEFT: *A stylized garland is delicately colored in shaded cherry red, harmonizing perfectly with the dusty pink ragged walls.*

Wallpaper and Paneling

From glorious multicolored floral prints to heavily embossed designs and gilded stripes, wallpaper provides color and textural interest, unifying and slightly softening wall surfaces. Both wallpaper and wood paneling, whether left plain, painted, or stained, add a little warmth to a room for a comfortable and cozy feel, as well as supplying a strong visual stimulus.

LEFT: *Crisp, tailored stripes above a chair rail papered with twining blue flowers suit the comfortable calm of a country house dining room.*

RIGHT: *Matching fabric doubles the impact of a French, traditional printed wallpaper, the faded pastoral pattern echoed and concentrated by the folds of the curtain.*

The Papered Room

Wallpaper gives a room a strong identity, a real sense of its character. The earliest papers, handpainted and later hand-printed, were very expensive, almost one-off works of art; mass production techniques have made wallpaper accessible to all pockets, and the range of style and quality is enormous.

The consistent repeatability of patterns printed on wallpaper is one of its most important characteristics, and designs are made to exploit it to the full. Traditional patterns, with realistic, figurative prints, heavy formal stripes, or repeated motifs, still have their place, particularly when choosing papers for a period scheme. More unusual and textured papers, and papers printed with foils or flocked and embossed, all offer alternative ways of decorating a wall.

Although it functions as a background, wallpaper is a dynamic medium, equally capable of grand statements and subtle effects.

BELOW: Stripes containing geometric patterns and floral designs in muted colors strike the appropriate period note in this elegant, high-ceilinged, Regency parlor.

LEFT: *A convincing printed representation of handmade, colorwashed paper looks exclusive and classy, with the convenience of simple paperhanging.*

RIGHT: *This casually striped contemporary wallpaper lives happily with floral printed fabric, and the simplicity of a split cane and check blind.*

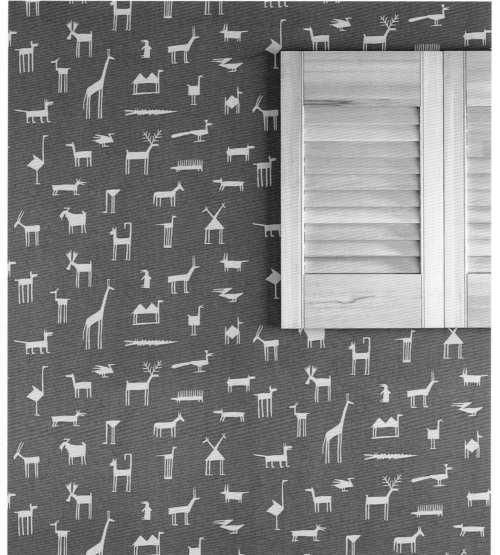

LEFT: *Primitively drawn birds and animals herd together on a rich, earthy red ground. Many wallpapers use the same repeat format.*

OPPOSITE: *Engravings repeated on a grand scale make a strikingly modern design.*

ABOVE: *Topiary is rendered in delicate watercolor, a beautifully balanced design for a sophisticated, contemporary effect.*

Wallpaper Update

Recent years have seen developments in paint and paper technology which have increased the potential variety of printed wallcoverings. The choice of imagery is ever-increasing, with photographic and computer-generated techniques encouraging complex and inventive products. The enthusiastic revival of painted decorative finishes has also led to the production of wallpapers printed in imitation of such techniques.

Wallpaper still performs the decorative function for which it was originally intended, and many old favorite classic designs are reprinted, year after year. Fresh new ideas keep coming, however, and there are many alternatives to traditional, sometimes rather overpowering, printed wallpapers.

Decoupage

A choice collection of cutout images pasted to a wall makes a great finishing touch, or an alternative to wallpaper. Decoupage is a richly decorative technique, developed in the eighteenth century, and it has many applications in contemporary schemes. Old printed images make excellent material for decoupage and there are many sourcebooks of copyright-free images available.

In fact, any kind of image may be used: catalog and magazine pages, family photographs, wrapping paper, even paintings and drawings. The thinner the paper, the better it will be for decoupage; if it is too thick, or if the image is the wrong size for its intended location, photocopies can be made to fit, in color or in black-and-white. Chosen images are carefully cut out with sharp scissors or a mat knife (scalpel), pasted in position, and varnished to protect their surface.

ABOVE: *Full-color copies of luscious fruits are used here for a fresh, exciting frieze; crisp color and orange border stripes against light green give the frieze a vibrant, contemporary look.*

LEFT: *Black-and-white engravings of farmyard animals have been photocopied, cut out, and arranged on the wall, a suitably rustic addition to this charming country kitchen.*

OPPOSITE: *Bold decoration striking an appropriate culinary note for a kitchen; colored copies were made of a picture of a carrot from an old seed catalog, cut out, and pasted onto deep blue, roughly painted walls.*

RIGHT: *This entire room has been decoupaged as a print room; yellow-washed walls are detailed with printed trompe l'oeil beaded paneling, chair rail, and frieze, while well-chosen ornithological prints are framed and linked with elegant paper cords and tassels.*

In the eighteenth century it was fashionable to make a print room, devoted to displaying collections of etchings and engravings, often of botanical or zoological subjects, or themes of antiquity. The prints were arranged and pasted on the walls in imitation of galleries containing painted pictures. The style can be re-created with black-and-white illustrations framed with elaborate paper borders, and festooned with swags, cords, and tassels; color can be added to the prints in imitation of early color printing and hand-finishing. Photocopies can be discreetly "aged" by dipping them in a weak solution of tea.

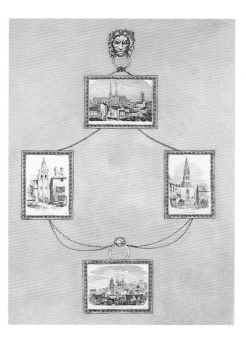

FAR LEFT: *Faded pale sepia colorwashing makes a perfect background for this series of prints of French villages. Uniform frame borders, and evenly looped cords held in a lion's mouth give a pleasing symmetry to the arrangement.*

LEFT: *Rather heavier in style than eighteenth-century prints, these Victorian engravings look rich and impressive displayed on softly stippled Venetian red walls. The weight and density of the images are well balanced by the robust background color.*

Applying Decoupage to a Wall

The wall should be marked with the position of the prints, measuring carefully, and checking straightness with a plumb line and spirit level. Either the print or the wall may be pasted, using clear-drying glue such as gum, starch paste, or wallpaper paste.

1 Apply glue to position marked on wall, spreading evenly with fingers to ensure an even coating.

2 Using both hands, position print, working across from edge to edge, smoothing to prevent bubbles forming.

3 With clean, damp sponge, wipe print outward from center, flattening creases and removing air bubbles.

4 Remove excess glue with damp sponge, repeating process as necessary. Glue residue can impair varnish adhesion.

5 Ensure edges and corners are firmly stuck. A few coats of varnish should be applied for protection.

Paper and paint, and no holds barred: a collection of printed chintzes is coordinated by color and tone, with floral wallpapers marshaled into formal panels framed by ragged paintwork, and accented with gray-green crown molding (cornice), chair rail, and baseboard.

267

ABOVE: Bathroom picket fencing; plain boards, cut with pointed tops, are brushed roughly with white and green eggshell paint, with sea-horses stenciled in a row near the top. The boards are battened away from the wall, casting attractive shadows.

Wood Paneling

For adding warmth and a comfortable, cozy feeling, wood paneling is a great choice. Paneling is not difficult to construct; it is simply fastened to wall battens, and the narrow width of the boards – plain butted, shiplap, or interlocking tongue-and-groove planking – means that it is easy to fit into any given space. It can also make excellent camouflage and insulation for pipework or uneven walls, the supporting battens being built out from the wall to the required distance, and the top completed with a shelf, creating a useful display or storage surface. The choice of finish depends on the effect required; most planed wood has varied grain, which looks lovely varnished or stained.

ABOVE: *Colorwashed milky-white paneling is topped with a bracketed shelf for plates, bright against a sea green wall.*

LEFT: *Plain boards are colorwashed in faded driftwood gray and sealed with clear, flat varnish, contrasting gently with glowing gold hardware.*

Colorwashing Wood

Colorwashing enhances the natural beauty of wood, emphasizing its varied texture. You can use transparent stains which will not obscure the grain of the wood and which are available in wood tones or bright colors. Alternatively, oil-based paint can be thinned with mineral spirits (white spirit) to make semi-opaque coatings.

1 *Seal knots in new wood using clear shellac knotting compound to prevent resins from spoiling the finish.*

2 *Thin two oil-based paint colors, 50:50 with mineral spirits (white spirit); apply darker color unevenly.*

3 *When first color is completely dry, apply second, unevenly, brushing out to avoid obvious lines.*

Painted Paneling

Wood has been used for centuries to make paneling, giving rise to some of the most skillful and exquisite decorative work. Carved panels simulating folded linen, or intricate geometric patterns, were installed in grand houses, waxed and burnished to a deep luster. Later, molded and painted plaster was introduced and added to wood, to make elegant neo-classical designs, embellished with moldings and painted and gilded. Paneling of this kind makes a decorative statement in its own right, but such exuberant styles do not suit all tastes.

More modest forms of paneling have always been used where there is need for a practical, good-looking means of both decorating a room, and protecting its walls from damage.

BELOW: Plates stand on a well-bracketed rail, atop warm red painted paneling turned neatly to make a window seat.

LEFT: *A soft woolen throw and a favorite armchair sit well against a wall, twin-striped with wallpaper and reeded-edge board paneling; warm chocolate-brown paint colors a cozy corner.*

ABOVE: *A wooden paneled seat is built into the window, painted and stenciled with motifs inspired by the Arts and Crafts movement; the border on the seat back continues around the room at the same height.*

Painted boarding makes handsome paneling, the various molded edges of different types of board contributing to the textural effect. Boards are usually fixed vertically, but they can just as easily be installed at other angles, making a feature of the direction of the planking.

As with any painted feature, the choice of finishes is vast, both textured and plain. High-gloss paint is very tough, but can look rather harsh and cold; flat finishes tend to mark easily and so needs protection with varnish; satin luster and eggshell paints are hardwearing, and both have a soft sheen, though slightly differing in character. The solid, straightforward look of boarded wooden paneling makes a strong statement in a room, defining and "anchoring" the boundaries, making the room feel welcoming and intimate.

Tiling

The colorful, durable nature of tiles has made them one of the most enduring means of decorating; their modular format gives great flexibility, allowing easy and inventive mixing of pattern, scale, and color. For kitchens or bathrooms, or for any walls exposed to water or steam, or which need to be easily cleaned, hard-glazed ceramic tiles make a practical and decorative choice.

LEFT: *A classic bathroom suite looks absolutely right against blue and white tiles bordered with a checkered frieze at chair rail and ceiling height.*

RIGHT: *Sheets of mosaic tiles make a neat but lively-textured waterproof wall, well-scaled for a small bathroom where larger tiles might look overpowering.*

ABOVE: Cheap and cheerful plain white tiles look jolly stamped with bright-colored starfish, a warm, sunny backsplash for a basin.

Bathroom Tiles

Tiled walls are hard-surfaced and unyielding, but with sympathetic use of color their precision and glaze make them look fresh and bright. Embossed or printed tiles add the texture of their pattern, used either all over or at regular or irregular intervals.

Combining tiles with contrasting materials gives interest and variety. They can be used to great effect in specific areas in a bathroom, most obviously as a backsplash behind a basin or a bath, or to define a shower area, the walls completed with perhaps cork, wood paneling, or a textured paint finish. Well-chosen accessories and ornaments add to the effect; glazed tiles look even brighter next to sea-scrubbed driftwood, seashells, and other flotsam and jetsam, set off with a welcoming pile of soft fluffy towels.

ABOVE: *Multicolored mosaic breakers wash over scallop shells, making an exuberant frieze above burnt orange tiles on a colorwashed wall.*

LEFT: *Ultramarine is stenciled roughly in a traditional pattern onto plain white tiles, enlivened with seaside treasures and rough timber.*

Mosaic

The ancient art of mosaic provides an individual way to add extra interest to your home. Like larger tiled surfaces, mosaics are tough and often brightly colored; and designs can be either figurative or abstract, sometimes incorporating bright metallic fragments to make surfaces glitter.

Any ceramic tiles can be used, cutting or breaking them into carefully sized or random shapes. Special sheets of mosaic pieces or tiles are widely available; small, opaque, colored glass pieces are mounted on paper, and slightly larger ceramic tiles on a mesh backing to allow for easy handling, especially for large areas of mosaic tiling in one color. The pieces are arranged and stuck into a layer of tile cement, then grouted to fill the gaps in between.

BELOW: A gentle wavy-topped backsplash is drawn with blocks of subtle heathery colors, bordered with peat brown.

ABOVE: Opaque glass mosaic pieces, in some of the extraordinary range of colors available on sheets, give designs a little lift.

ABOVE: Each piece is cut roughly into quarters with tile cutters; a paper pattern helps to determine how much mosaic is needed for each part of the design.

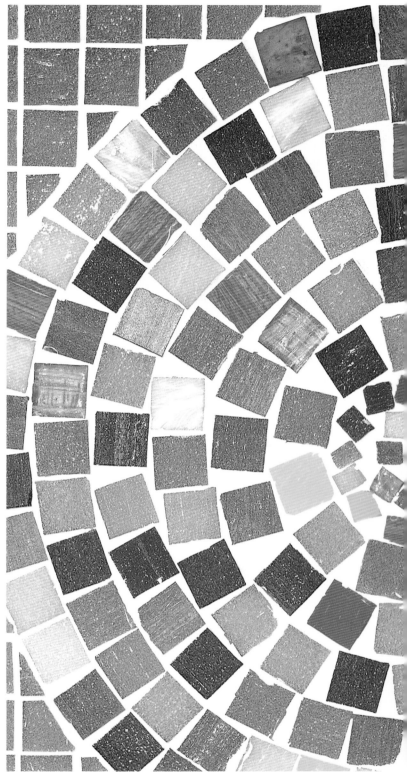

ABOVE: Casually squared mosaic pieces, large and small, in jewel-like colors and a simple geometric arrangement, make a brilliant tabletop design.

Kitchen Tiles

The same washability and sturdiness which make tiles so suited to bathroom use make them just as good for kitchens, and for other useful rooms like larders, mudrooms, and laundries. In addition, the coldness of glazed or unglazed ceramic tiles helps keep worktops cool, ideal for bread and pastry making.

Not all tiles are brightly glazed; there are dozens of different finishes, from smooth, hard engineering tiles and soft, terra-cotta-colored quarries, through the infinite range of printed and embossed tiles with every imaginable kind of image or texture, to handmade tiles, salt-glazed or individually painted – something to please every taste. Antique tiles from different periods are enthusiastically collected; tiles brought home from foreign countries make lovely permanent vacation souvenirs, to be fitted into the tiling of a kitchen wall. Mixing texture and pattern, pictorial content and style, can produce exciting results. Many kitchen-themed designs for tiles are available, with culinary imagery to the fore; they can look very good, given either a restrained approach or else the full, over-the-top treatment. Tiled walls tend to look busy, though the intensity of an all-over scheme, particularly in a small kitchen, often creates a really dynamic effect.

OPPOSITE: The kitchen at Giverny, where the painter Claude Monet lived, still has its magnificent cast-iron range and original blue-and-white Rouen tiles.

BELOW: Handmade blue and rust tiles sit perfectly with a wooden sideboard, roughly plastered walls, and a butler's sink.

Decorating Tiles

For a truly personal and unique touch, it is easy to decorate tiles using simple printing techniques like stamping and stenciling; the strength of a hand-printed design makes a striking contribution to a decorative scheme, and it is fun and very satisfying to produce something really appropriate and original.

Plain white glazed tiles are cheap and easily available, and make an excellent background for all colors, but there is no reason why striking decoration should not be successfully applied to any plain colored tiles, glazed or unglazed. As well as potatoes, familiar from childhood printing, many materials may be used to make stamps: paperboard (card), polystyrene or styrofoam, linoleum – anything which can be cut into patterns will do. Stamping gives a pleasantly varied result; color is painted or rolled onto the stamp which is then pressed firmly onto the tile. Acrylic or oil-based color is suitable for stamping, and for stenciling, for which cellulose spray paint for cars also works well. However, for durable results, tile paint, or at least tile primer, works best.

ABOVE: *Six stenciled tiles, showing simple multicolored designs painted in softly graded colors – fresh pretty images, with naive charm.*

RIGHT: *Bold, simple drawings of peppers, stamped alternately in red and green, make a perfect backdrop in a kitchen.*

OPPOSITE: *This stylish treatment uses corner-stamped tiles for a strong all-over pattern, varied with bold stenciled cockerels.*

Floors

The floor is a large area of color and texture which fundamentally influences the overall feel of a room. Wooden boards and tiles are excellent flooring materials and linoleum and vinyl, once thought of as cheap substitutes for traditional materials, are now made in a vast range of styles and qualities, some convincingly replicating natural wood or stone, some in unique patterns and textures.

LEFT: *Warm, resilient vinyl flooring, in patterns faithfully imitating natural materials, is used for a businesslike kitchen and the elegant dining room beyond.*

RIGHT: *Fake granite setts are stamped in oil-based paint on white vinyl tiles, for a budget-priced and waterproof, mosaic-effect bathroom floor.*

Beautiful Bare Boards

A wooden floor, old or new, has great warmth and beauty. A natural, resilient, and flexible material, wood ages most attractively, darkening with exposure to sunlight, and slowly accumulating the marks, scars, and patina of traffic.

The gently varied color of timber, and the rhythmic pattern of neatly laid boards, have a pleasing vitality, making a neutral base for furnishings. The colors and grains of different woods are distinctive, lending themselves perfectly to transparent stained and polished finishes. Varnishes are available in varying degrees of gloss; waxes need frequent reapplication and polishing, but the resulting shine is subtle and well worth the effort.

Boarded wooden flooring can be formal and polished, invisibly ("secret") nailed, and very expensive. Cheap construction timber, or bargain-priced timber reclaimed from redundant buildings, makes excellent flooring, with a rough-and-ready character which mellows gently with wear-and-tear.

BELOW: This dark, narrow-boarded, polished floor makes a unifying background for a bold woven rug and seagrass-upholstered settle.

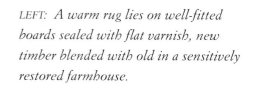

LEFT: A warm rug lies on well-fitted boards sealed with flat varnish, new timber blended with old in a sensitively restored farmhouse.

BELOW: Wide oak boards in a formal dining room make solid underpinnings for tartans and striped curtains.

BOTTOM: In this study, rugged, well-worn elm floorboards gleam softly with the patina of age.

Stenciling on Wood Floors

Clean-cut stenciled designs look wonderful on wooden floors; their strong graphic quality is particularly effective, being bold enough not to be overshadowed by the grain of the wood, nor broken up by the joins between planks or wood blocks.

Transparent colored varnishes and colored wood stains are very effective for stenciling on clean new wood, as they soak deeply into the timber, enhancing the grain, which glows softly through the color. Old boards are attractive, but their surfaces are often dark and marked so that transparent colors are less successful. In such cases, denser acrylic color works well, or the wood can be sanded to smooth and clean the surface.

Stenciled patterns look great in rooms where there is little furniture to obscure the painting. The most effective results are achieved with strong, simple designs, often based on geometric or traditional folk art motifs, using perhaps one color predominantly, with a second or third for interest and impact.

RIGHT: A rhythmic border pattern taken from a design by William Morris: brownish-black stenciled leaves, highlighted with crimson fuchsias.

OPPOSITE: Stained in green and indigo, diamonds and triangles make a stylish board-width pattern, with corners punctuated by naive flowers.

The pattern of the floor itself can be helpful in planning a design, using the board widths or block pattern repeat as a grid measurement to position the stencils. Designs can be devised especially to exploit specific block patterns like herringbone or basketweave parquet, with striking results.

Ambitious trompe l'oeil designs can also be stenciled, with hand-drawn and painted details added for a more lifelike effect: a richly patterned oriental rug, perhaps, with fringes and maybe one corner folded back as though it had been kicked up accidentally. Or it could be fun to have a chessboard, a hopscotch grid, or snakes-and-ladders stenciled on a playroom floor. Whatever the design, the whole floor, including the finished stenciled work, should be coated at least twice with clear flat varnish for protection. It can then be safely polished without damaging the decoration.

RIGHT: A three-colored design in a simplified version of a classical pattern makes a lively border; warm yellow ocher and persimmon red complement the beautifully grained floorboards, a fresh but subtle effect.

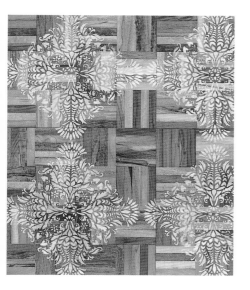

LEFT: A single white, stippled motif, grouped in fours, puts a new slant on a basketweave parquet floor.

RIGHT: Trios of chickens in deep Indian red are brush-stenciled onto a pale birchwood block floor, for a dramatic, almost abstract effect.

Cutting a Stencil

A carefully cut stencil gives the best results. Books of ready-printed designs are widely available, printed on paperboard (card), which should be made resistant to paint, particularly if using water-based color. The stencil may then be cut out and printed, easily wiped clean, and reused.

1 Make stencil paint-proof, dabbing with boiled linseed oil and turpentine mixed 50:50. Dry for ten minutes.

2 Cut out stencil around design, using sharp mat knife (scalpel) on self-healing cutting mat.

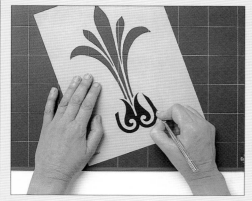

3 Keep knife at constant angle, moving paperboard (card) around under blade to give smooth-cut stencil edges.

4 Clean stencil edges aid good prints; work steadily, changing blades frequently to ensure good cutting.

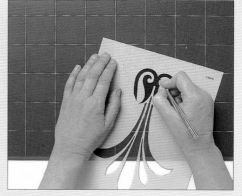

5 Rotate paperboard (card) for smooth curves. By using a cutting mat you can avoid skips and glitches.

ABOVE: *Beautiful mellow original stone tiles in pale honey and terra-cotta have the soft patina of many years of wear, the perfect floor for this timbered room.*

Floor Tiles

For every type of room and decor, there are tiles to suit the floor: elegant marble, laid in classic checkerboard patterns; resilient textured rubber or vinyl for a modern industrial feel; cut stone or molded ceramic; cork; even carpet tiles.

Tough ceramic tiles, in finishes imitating stone, or in plain colors and myriad patterns, make floors of distinctive character and charm. They are particularly popular in hot countries where cool stone or ceramic mosaic floors are not only beautiful but also a welcome relief from the heat. Plain square tiles make a surface with a gridded texture created by the joins between the tiles. This can be almost invisible, or exaggerated, depending on how closely the tiles are laid. The joins can be made into a feature, with contrast-colored grouting or with inserts between them. Marble, in all its rainbow range of colors, makes floors which are often grand and formal, polished to a glass-like finish. Granite, limestone, and slate are less dramatically colored and easy to live with, and they wear gradually to a soft sheen, their subtle neutral colors flattering to the rest of the room.

ABOVE: *A checkerboard of old red and brown quarry tiles has been lovingly polished, its colors glowing gently with age.*

LEFT: *Smooth stone flags, laid with wide joins and sealed with polish, make a characterful floor, its color picked up in the curtain fabric.*

Decorated Furniture

A well-decorated room deserves equally lovely furniture. Whether plain or unfinished, simply old or worn, any furniture can be revitalized with a decorative finish, even just a carefully applied coat of paint.

A decoration project could be an extensive revamp of an entire suite of furniture, or a quick and simple facelift for a well-worn favorite table or chair.

LEFT: *A corner cupboard, hutch (dresser), and plate rack are colorwashed in muted green and turquoise and subtly distressed – a delicious backdrop for pastel luster china.*

RIGHT: *This gateleg table was stenciled with peaches, stippled in delicate gradated color over thinned washes of off-white and almond green.*

LEFT: *A plain cupboard gets dramatic. Panels are boldly woodgrained through cream eggshell over chalky blue – stunning against the subtly colorwashed wall.*

OPPOSITE: *Bright pastel cherubs in a graphic style adorn green-washed cabinets.*

ABOVE: *A carefully masked border painted on the drawer fronts is emphasized with stenciled cords and tassels, a light, pretty, and original treatment.*

Paint Effects

A lot of furniture has flat areas which cry out for decoration. From simple colored patterns to rich, varied textures and realistic pictures, there are paint effects to achieve whatever decorative result is desired.

It is a good idea to prepare the surface to be decorated by sanding it; this will smooth out any lumps or bumps, and if the furniture is already painted, polished, or varnished, will abrade the surface, keying it so that a new base layer of paint will adhere well. Cupboard doors and drawer fronts make great canvases for trompe l'oeil and other pictorial treatments. There are many sources for illustration ideas, such as magazines and books full of images which can be copied or traced onto furniture and then painted.

RIGHT: *This sideboard was dragged, the carcass once, the panels and drawer twice, at right angles.*

OPPOSITE: *Delicate, stylized birds and trees on an antiqued background decorate the paneled doors of this gray-green cupboard.*

ABOVE: *Close-toned rag rolling decorates the drawer fronts of this chest of drawers.*

The whole gamut of painting techniques can be used to decorate furniture, mixing and matching to great effect.

Different treatments can be applied to the different parts of a piece; for example, the carcass and drawers of a chest, or the panels of cupboard doors. Suites of furniture, such as dining tables and chairs, could be decorated with coordinated or counterchanged effects, the tabletop and chair seats in one finish, all the legs in subtly different textures, or closely related colors. Careful choice, of both the effects and the colors, is important, to avoid over-complicating the look. Colors of similar strength and tone work well together, but even very disparate colors can be combined and coated with a textured glaze for an unusual, variegated effect.

ABOVE: Brilliant orange nasturtiums scramble around this trusty chest, stenciled in acrylic onto a freely painted background of pale, cloudy gray.

Stenciling onto Furniture

It is very easy to adapt or build up stencil designs to fit a variety of shapes; small and portable items of furniture – trunks, occasional tables, stools – become special treasures with the addition of a stenciled decoration. Bold, simplified, or stylized stenciled images can be printed in sequence to make wonderful friezes and borders, and surfaces can be scattered with repeated motifs, giving a new lease of life to tired furniture. A single image, perhaps linked to other furnishings, can add a whole new dimension to a room.

ABOVE: Stenciled cherubs blow a fanfare, stationed at each end of an existing rose garland decal.

ABOVE LEFT: A vigorous, beautifully executed border, edged with gold, is exquisite decoration for a black-painted table in an elegant dining room.

LEFT: A lively pattern of lemon branches is stenciled onto a sturdy kitchen table.

Painted furniture has a particularly approachable quality, the vibrance and energy of color giving otherwise quite solid and heavy-looking pieces an air of gaiety and lightness. Stenciling adds a subtle touch of order to painted decoration by virtue of its neat, firm edges and controlled, repeatable patterns. With a number of separate stencils combined, complex designs can be applied to large and complicated pieces of furniture, using the stencil images in various groupings, or singly, and in conjunction with plain colors painted as backgrounds, or to highlight parts of the piece.

Oil-based color can be used to stencil furniture that is used out of doors. Wood stains can also be stenciled, though it is necessary with some types of stain to apply a sealant over the first coat if subsequent coatings are not to spread into it unevenly. The whole design can also be sealed when it is complete. Wood stains and preservatives, for horticultural and general outdoor use, are available in a wide range of natural wood tones, and increasingly in a variety of bright colors.

With any stenciling, the success of the result depends on the stencil itself being cut and positioned carefully, and the color being applied with as much imagination as skill.

RIGHT: A rocking chair is given a pretty, traditional look with a trail of flowers stenciled on the seat and elements echoed on the chair back.

OPPOSITE: Three stencils are combined to decorate this bench, using bold primary colors, blended and flat, for a highly ornamented effect.

Liming

Several methods of decorating wood exploit its natural grain pattern. Liming imitates the old custom of painting wooden furniture with diluted limewash left over from painting the walls in farmhouses. Now, instead of using limewash, liming wax (a mixture of beeswax and whiting) is worked into the wood and the surface is polished, leaving a residue of white wax in the grain. The effect is light and pretty, working best on wood that has a strong, fairly open and linear grain patternm such as oak.

Liming can revitalize heavy, dark old furniture, making it look fresh and contemporary; the same process can also be applied to light-colored wood for a different contrast, using wax mixed with colored pigments, emphasizing the grain with black or perhaps a deep earthy red.

BELOW: A limed finish gives these modern kitchen cabinets a comfortable, time-worn look, emphasizing their soft color and pretty grain.

LEFT: *Once shrouded with gloomy brown polish, this little chest has been stripped and limed, revealing the robust texture of oak.*

Liming

Liming is a straightforward process, but for the best results good preparation is important. If liming is to be applied to old furniture, all traces of heavy sealed or polished finishes must be completely removed, and even with new wood, the surface should be sanded until smooth and clean.

1 Work wire brush in direction of grain, removing soft wood, emphasizing grain.

2 Apply liming wax generously with fine steel wool, along and across grain.

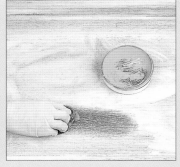

3 Leave for 30 minutes. Remove liming wax with steel wool and wax polish.

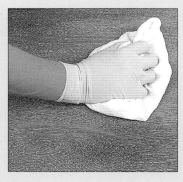

4 Polish cleared surface with soft cotton cloth; polish occasionally with clear wax.

Waxing, Woodgraining, and Staining

The natural pattern of wood grain looks best given a clear finish. Beeswax is a popular wax for furniture, polishing to a rich, mellow sheen. Waxes may be colored with pigments, used either to enrich natural wood tones, or worked into the grain and moldings of a piece of furniture, then polished, leaving residual color in the wood.

Artificial graining creates textural interest on woods with insignificant grain; it is also used simply to fake a particular wood, such as bird's eye maple, burr elm, or walnut, by laying glazes and drawing into them in the pattern of the grain. Oak graining gives a less subtle look; glazes are laid over cream paint, then combed to imitate oak's distinctive straight grain.

Stains can be layered, and for interesting effects they can be sanded to reveal previous layers, or even back to bare wood.

ABOVE: *A new, unpainted chair has been stained, first pink, then with green, and rubbed back to reveal the pink in places.*

LEFT: *This detail shows bright stain colors applied to the carving, layered and rubbed back repeatedly for a rich, multicolored finish.*

ABOVE: *Thick dark varnish was stripped off this old wooden headboard and it was then covered with a layer of white wax.*

LEFT: *Brush swirls and layers of dabbed on glaze were use to imitate the pattern of Bird's eye maple on this pine mirror frame.*

Antiquing

Most methods of antiquing furniture involve applying paint layers which are subsequently broken down ("distressed") by sanding, polishing, or even hitting, revealing traces of color or bare wood. Crackle glaze uses a special medium to create the look of peeling paint, while crackle varnish combines two varnishes to get a crazed finish. Whatever method is chosen, the treated surface can be coated with tinted wax and buffed, leaving color ingrained in cracks and brush marks like the grime of ages.

These finishes can be applied to old or new wood, but a smooth sanded surface gives more predictable results. Applied to furniture decorated in a period style, antiquing produces some attractive and convincing results.

RIGHT: The light, Italianate look of this chair was achieved by incising patterns through wet paint and also by wiping the paint from the moldings to reveal an under layer of gold.

LEFT: *Off-white paint, roughly applied, with a little blue around the handles and gilt cream smeared over terra-cotta all around the edges, is waxed with transparent brown, and buffed to a gentle sheen.*

Crackle-Finish Antiquing

Crackle varnishing uses an oil-based varnish applied over a basecoat. When touch-dry, the varnish is coated with a quicker-drying, water-based varnish, the different drying rates making the second coat craze. The peeling paint effect shown here uses crackle glaze medium over latex (emulsion) paint.

1 Sand, prime, and paint surface, using latex (emulsion) paint; rub down between coats for a smooth finish.

2 When base paint is dry, apply thin layer of crackle glaze to panels. Leave to dry.

3 Apply latex (emulsion), painting panels last and working quickly as paint on panels rapidly starts crackling.

4 When top coat is dry, sand areas of paint to imitate the effects of wear-and-tear.

5 Rub with very diluted brown paint using fine steel wool, lightly tinting and distressing the overall finish.

Gilded Furniture

There is nothing which quite matches the unmistakable gleam of gold. Gilding adds a touch of brilliance, luxurious and extravagant, transfiguring a humble piece of furniture.

Gold can be applied to most materials, and it is available in several different forms. Beaten into air-thin sheets, real gold leaf is the brightest of all, but Dutch metal, which is brass in leaf form, makes an excellent alternative. Sheet metals are applied to a surface coated with gold size, a special glue which is transparent when dry. Bronze powders, finely ground from gold-colored metals, are similarly applied, dusted densely or in light sprinklings onto the size. Gilt creams and waxes are ready-mixed preparations in a range of different-colored golds, easily applied with brushes or fingers, then buffed when dry to a lustrous finish. Apart from real gold, gilt finishes will tarnish in time, so should be protected with clear varnish.

BELOW: A simple chest of drawers is transformed. Deep sea washes of sand-sprinkled blues and turquoise are swept with gold leaf, blistered by the uneven paint surface.

ABOVE: *Broken tints in autumn golds; size, roller-printed through a stencil, is dusted with bronze powders for a variegated effect.*

LEFT: *Patterns drawn with a cork through wet white paint reveal shimmering gold leaf on the drawers of this little chest.*

Decoupaged Furniture

Decoupage is a wonderful decorative treatment for furniture, endlessly adaptable to its various shapes, from chair legs to headboards and beyond.

Well-executed decoupage is extremely durable, making it suitable for such hard-working furniture as tables and chairs. The surface should ideally be finished absolutely smooth, the edges of the cutout images undetectable to the touch. This is achieved by applying numerous coats of clear varnish or lacquer, rubbing down between coats with very fine wet-and-dry sandpaper, building a glasslike finish. Of course, it can also be effective to allow the collaged paper texture to be evident, even becoming a feature of the design. Decoupage is frequently used to create a period look, but that can mean any period – contemporary images decoupaged on furniture, on their own or mixed with older pictures, have a vitality and immediacy which are very attractive.

LEFT: Distressed, colorwashed paint makes a lively background for roughly cut images, creating a vigorous effect in well-chosen colors.

OPPOSITE: Subtle landscape colors make a painterly background for a decoupaged eighteenth-century country scene, elegantly framed by the headboard molding.

ABOVE: *Part of a magnificent decoupaged headboard trimmed with woven braid. Portraits, animals, manuscripts, and flowers jostle together, in a riot of color.*

LEFT: *Decoupaged wrapping paper makes "inlaid" oriental birds and malachite panels, imitating eighteenth-century lacquered furniture.*

OPPOSITE: *Panels with gothic arched tops form a portable "print room" screen in the classic decoupage style.*

Children's Furniture

Color is probably the first thing children notice about anything. Furniture for children should be functional, colorful, and, above all, fun.

Most children's furniture has a hard life, so paint finishes should be both tough and easy to clean; a chest of drawers may have to double as a climbing frame, or pretend train, so it will need all the help it can get. Small children put just about everything into their mouths at some time or other, so it is essential to use non-toxic, lead-free paints for their furniture, just in case.

Strong colors look good in a child's room. Plain colors coordinate well and make an easy background for the jumble of toys and clothes. Techniques like stenciling and decoupage are great fun too, using simple designs and pictures of favorite objects, toys, or fictional characters.

BELOW: A big wooden chest, solidly painted in shiny blue and yellow, makes a perfect toy box.

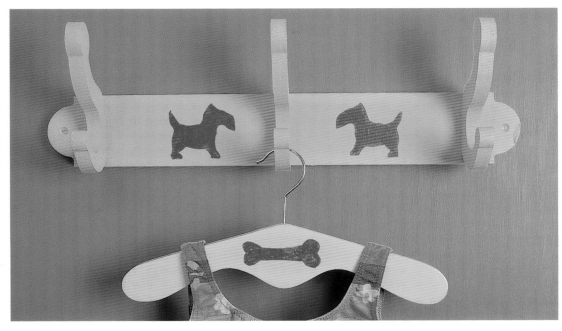

ABOVE: *Drawers painted in different colors make it easier to remember whose things live where in a shared bedroom.*

LEFT: *Not forgetting the details: a chunky coat rack and hanger are stenciled with good dogs and a bone.*

Directory

The best results are achieved with good materials and equipment, persistence, and imagination. While enthusiasm and experiment overcome many difficulties, a little guidance about how materials work together is useful. On the following pages are some examples of the different types of paint and their colors as well as information on stains, waxes, and varnishes.

LEFT: *The fruits of the decorator's labors: paint effects, decoupage, gilding, or antiquing, used individually or combined, produce an infinity of riches.*

RIGHT: *All set to go, with freshly mixed color, clean brush, and sharp knife. Using good materials is half the enjoyment of decorating with paint.*

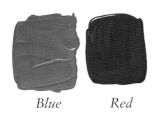

Blue   *Red*

Yellow   *White*

Paint Colors and Mixing Paint

A little basic color theory: the primary colors are red, yellow, and blue. With these, plus white and black, most other colors can be mixed. There are warm colors (sunshine yellow, orange, red, red-purple) and cool colors (blue-violet, blue, green, lemon yellow). Colors of the same temperature (warm or cool), or the same tone (dark or light), harmonize; complementary colors – opposing colors within the warm and cool groups, such as sunshine yellow and blue-violet – and colors of opposite temperature or tone, can be used for emphasis or contrast.

Orange (yellow plus red) plus white makes pale orange.

Strong dark red plus white makes Old Rose pink.

Light red (red plus yellow) plus white makes terra-cotta.

Blue plus white makes pale, ice blue.

Green (blue plus yellow) plus white makes almond green.

Yellow plus a little red makes a light orange.

Red plus a little yellow makes a terra-cotta red.

Red plus blue makes dull purple.

Purple (red plus blue) plus white makes soft lilac.

Green (blue plus yellow) plus red and white makes fawn.

Yellow plus a little blue makes lime green.

Blue plus a little yellow makes blue-green.

Blue plus a little red makes indigo blue.

Purple (red plus blue) plus yellow and white makes taupe.

Orange (yellow plus red) plus white and blue makes olive.

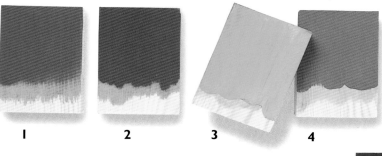

1 **2** **3** **4**

LEFT: *Reds.* **1** *Deep red; intense clear color, warm, deep.* **2** *Indian red; warm, darkened with umber.* **3** *Rose pink; white adds opacity, lightens color.* **4** *Terra-cotta; warm, brownish; deep reds recede visually, contrast with greens.*

RIGHT: *Blues.* **1** *Spectrum blue; clear, "neutral" blue, warm.* **2** *Duck egg blue; warm dense pastel.* **3** *Gray-blue; white lightens, black cools slightly.* **4** *Prussian blue; intense, greenish.*

1 **2** **3** **4**

LEFT: *Yellows.* **1** *Golden yellow; advances visually, clear, cool.* **2** *Yellow ocher; "dirtied" with brown, soft, warm.* **3** *Raw sienna; natural earthy color, warm, neutral.* **4** *Olive khaki; green-brown.*

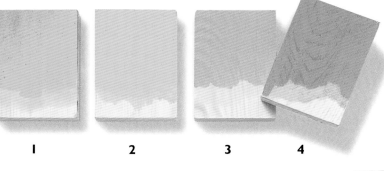

1 **2** **3** **4**

RIGHT: *Greens.* **1** *Prussian green; intense, cool blue-green.* **2** *Mid-green; cool, muted with blue.* **3** *Gray-green; white adds opacity and warmth.* **4** *Dark olive; warm brownish green.*

1 **2** **3** **4**

LEFT: *Browns.* **1** *Light sepia; cool, neutral.* **2** *Pale sienna; reddish, lightened with white.* **3** *Burnt sienna; rich, natural red-brown, warm.* **4** *Dark brown; deep, clear, warm.*

1 **2** **3** **4**

RIGHT: *Neutrals.* **1** *Off-white; cool, gray tinge, opaque.* **2** *Cool gray; sepia added.* **3** *French gray; reddish brown added, warm.* **4** *Payne's gray; intense, blue-black, cool.*

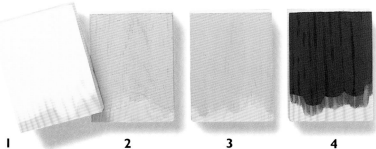

1 **2** **3** **4**

Catalog of Paint Effects

While the textures of paint effects are obviously quite distinct from each other, a single technique carried out in different colorways can look strikingly different.

Simple reversals, light on dark with dark on light, used together create variety in a decorative scheme. Techniques can easily be made to look either bold or subtle by using colors with more or less contrast. The samples shown here give a few color ideas to consider; the colors used are mostly quite strong, with pronounced contrast.

Very strong contrast looks dramatic, showing the pattern of the paint effect very clearly; combinations in close tones, or shades of one color, give a more discreet result. It is also interesting to use more than one pattern layer, and not necessarily with the same pattern repeated. Bold-patterned effects look good over smaller-scale textures, ragging over colorwashing or sponging, or decorative graining on a stippled base coat.

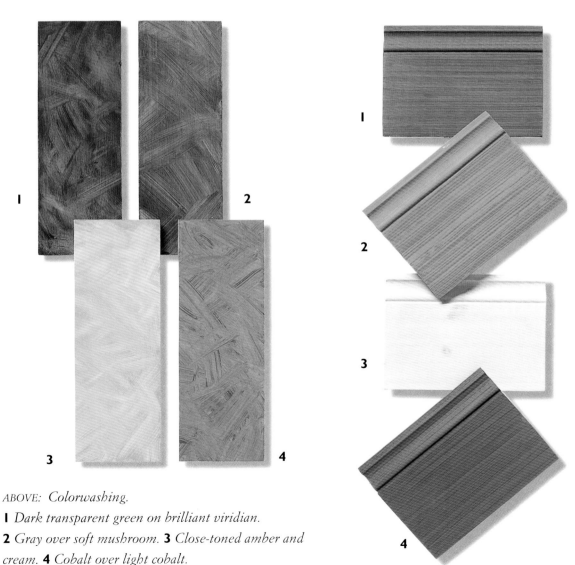

ABOVE: *Colorwashing.*
1 *Dark transparent green on brilliant viridian.*
2 *Gray over soft mushroom.* **3** *Close-toned amber and cream.* **4** *Cobalt over light cobalt.*

ABOVE: *Sponging.*
1 *Dark green and stone over buff.* **2** *Black over blue.*
3 *Ocher on rich red.*
4 *Red over green.*

LEFT: *Dragging.*
1 *Classic, dark on light green.* **2** *Terra-cotta over pink.* **3** *Translucent white over varnish.* **4** *Transparent black over brick red.*

BELOW: *Decorative graining.*
1 *Nearly natural-looking transparent brown, with dark brown graining.*
2 *Light on dark blue, a watered-silk effect.* **3** *Fresh green on yellow, strong contrast.* **4** *Bold pinks, dark on light.*

BELOW: *Frottage.*
1 *Marine blue on red, a rich combination.* **2** *Delicate ripples of translucent off-white paint traced over pale, ice blue.* **3** *Deep green over turquoise, like malachite.*
4 *Dramatic scarlet on Prussian green.*

ABOVE: *Ragging.*
1 *Dark red ragged over soft pearly gray.* **2** *Bottle green ragged over a base of mint green and viridian.* **3** *Ocher over terra-cotta, rich, oriental coloring.* **4** *Cool dark blue on white.*

ABOVE: *Stippling.*
1 *Deep ultramarine stippled over rich rose pink.*
2 *A soft Mediterranean blue stippled over pale lemon yellow, warm and velvety.*
3 *Deep, warm cherry on burnt orange.* **4** *Somber, dark on mid- green.*

Wood Staining and Painting

Paint is ideal for covering and sealing, and for leveling unevenness, such as wood grain. Most paint, oil-based or water-based, is opaque, unless thinned considerably; thinned paint soaks into wood, making a good first coating for a really smooth opaque finish. It is also ideal for distressing and revealed-wood effects, where wood grain shows through in places. Wood stain is much thinner, either water-based or solvent-based, an intensely colored transparent coating which soaks well into wood.

The color of transparent stains is affected by the type and color of wood used; on hardwoods stains are less brilliant than on light softwoods like pine. Paint can be applied over stain, which, unless it is very thinned, it will obscure; stain applied over paint affects the color of both paint and wood.

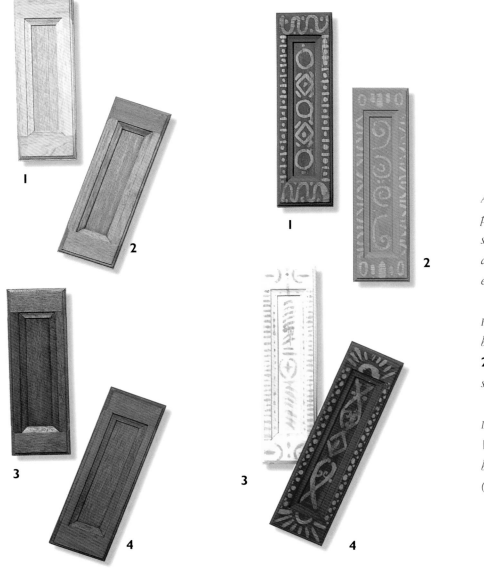

ABOVE: Painting and distressing on pine. **I** *Gray latex (emulsion), wiped, sanded.* **2** *Chalky blue latex (emulsion), distressed.* **3** *Sanded terra-cotta eggshell.* **4** *Palest blue, distressed.*

FAR LEFT: Using modern stains on beech. **I** *Plain, unstained, pale pinkish.* **2** *Dilute blue stain.* **3** *Teak, water-based stain.* **4** *Red stain, water-based.*

LEFT: Revealing pine under paint. **I** *Thinned green eggshell paint.* **2** *Light blue latex (emulsion).* **3** *White latex (emulsion).* **4** *Thinned dark red.*

BELOW: **I** *Pine, black painted design under clear oil-based sealant.* **2** *Acrylic-painted design on pine, sealed with acrylic.* **3** *Mahogany water-based stain, colorless water-based sealant.*

BELOW: **I** *Pine, design stenciled and drawn in water-based paint, clear sealed.* **2** *Black stain over red stain on mahogany.* **3** *Mahogany, stained and sealed with lightly pigment-tinted oil-based sealant.*

ABOVE: **I** *Pine, water-based green paint.* **2** *Mahogany, stained, sealed.* **3** *Mahogany, dark oil-based stain.*

ABOVE: **I** *Pine, diluted water-based blue paint.* **2** *Clear-sealed pine.* **3** *Mahogany, water-based blue paint design, oil-based sealant.*

LEFT: *Samples of light pine and darker mahogany; horizontal strips of paint overlaid with vertical strips of stain, comparing the effects of different colored stains on bare wood and painted colors, light and dark. Stains have stronger effect on lighter-colored wood and paint.*

unstained   *yellow*   *red*   *dark brown*   *blue*   *black*

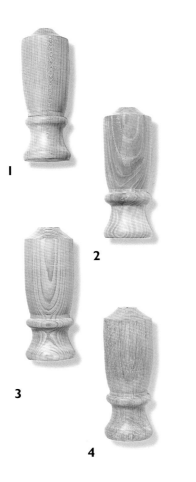

Waxing

The subtle sheen of waxed furniture has a rich and timeless quality which suits any style or period of decor. A polished wax finish is particularly sympathetic on wood, bringing out the color and pattern of its grain, and giving a softly glossy finish with a pleasant, smooth feel, which is also excellent for painted finishes on wooden or metal furniture.

There are waxes, both synthetic and natural, for many different decorative purposes. In addition to clear waxes and light, naturally colored waxes like beeswax for protective polishing, there are soft, colored waxes to match wood tones, for finishing and restoring, and dark waxes for antiquing effects, worked deep into grain and moldings. White wax, a mixture of beeswax and whiting powder, is used for liming. Clear waxes may be tinted with any pigment to make colored wax for exciting effects, stenciling or direct coloring, or color variations of techniques such as liming.

A waxed finish is not entirely durable, but it is fairly waterproof and can in any case be brought back to good condition by rewaxing and polishing. Though not as tough as some varnished or hard painted finishes, wax-polished furniture has a soft, glowing quality, a beautiful finish with the added bonus of a pleasant, subtle perfume.

ABOVE: **1** *Liming on elm.* **2** *White wax on ash.* **3** *Limed and polished pine.* **4** *White wax on close-grained oak.*

LEFT: *Subtle sheen and minimal color change make clear wax a good choice for wood and furniture. Less brilliantly shiny than gloss varnish, its lustrous finish is more lively than flat varnish; it is less tough but still offers some degree of surface protection.*

LEFT: *With the same protective properties and quality of shine as clear wax, dark wax is used for antiquing, worked into the surface and moldings of furniture and other decorative details, and polished to leave a residue of simulated grime.*

LEFT: *Pine board with horizontal strips of paint (top to bottom: light blue, off-white, olive green, dark red, and untreated pine) overlaid with vertical bands of different waxes (left to right: untreated, clear wax, reddish wax, yellow wax, mid-brown wax, dark wax, and blue-tinted clear wax) shows the effects of different wax finishes on bare wood and painted colors.*

Varnishing

The traditional clear, hard finish for wood is varnish. Varying in color from pale yellow to almost black, oil-based varnish is flexible and durable, suited to both old wood and new, and it gives a high degree of protection from the ravages of sunlight. The slight yellowing of traditional varnish is not unattractive, enriching and deepening colors over which it is painted. Most traditional and oil-based varnishes are slow to dry, taking several hours, apart from shellac, which is made with denatured alcohol (methylated spirits) and dries in minutes. Shellac is useful as a waterproof sealant, but it is slightly brittle.

Modern, water-based acrylic varnishes are faster-drying than oil-based and are available in a truly colorless form, which is useful when a clean, bright, surface is to be coated without altering the colors. Most varnishes, traditional and modern, are available in gloss, satin, or semigloss, and matte or flat finishes, although it is hard to find a truly flat, oil-based varnish. All types of varnish may be tinted with pigment or oil color, and there is an ever-widening range of colored, ready-mixed varnishes, water-based and quick-drying, which can be used to create exciting multicolored, layered effects. Strong, clear colors can be intermixed, and also used as glazes in decorative painted effects.

LEFT: *Colored varnishes.* **1** *Oak, checks in terra-cotta, blue, green, and purple.* **2** *Pale figured sycamore shimmers through checked browns, pale pink, green, mauve, and blue.* **3** *The strong pattern and color of pitch pine are matched by blues, terra-cotta, and green.* **4** *Subdued colors are lifted with white and blue, on red, fine-grained mahogany.*

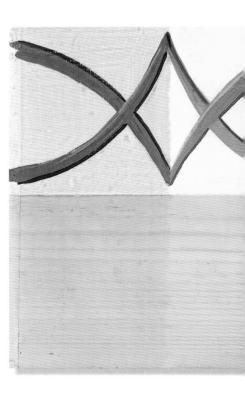

Introduction

Successful decoration is the result of a happy marriage between your initial design and the extras that confirm your decorating style. Atmospheric lighting, practical and good-looking storage, and the art of displaying plants and accessories are all considered.

LEFT: *Careful attention to details, from well-chosen furniture and lighting for daytime and evening to welcoming vases of wildflowers, creates a spirit of harmony.*

RIGHT: *Storage can be decorative as well as practical, especially in the kitchen.*

ABOVE: *Clever juggling with space provides sleeping quarters for three children in a high-ceilinged room, with light and air from the small high window. The balustrade, essential for safety, adds decorative interest.*

Clever Organization

Successful homemaking depends on tailoring and using space according to our needs, which vary enormously. The same apartment might be arranged entirely differently by friends sharing, by a couple, or by a family. Moreover, it could well need adjusting as its occupants' lives change. For instance, small children need parental attention all the time, whereas teenagers want somewhere to hide. Or perhaps someone has joined the growing ranks of people who work from home. Life changes demand allowances in the way you arrange your space at home.

Most of us would like more living space – yet conversely, many of us actually have more than we use. If you have high ceilings, could you be using vertical space in the form of a platform for sleeping or working? There might be room for a desk in that awkward space under the stairs. Clever organization and lateral thinking are more important than the number of fitted cupboards you possess.

CLEVER ORGANIZATION

LEFT: *A reclaimed glass-drawered shop unit becomes time-saving bedroom storage, showing everything that is needed at a glance. A large-scale, distinctive piece of furniture like this adds character and focus to the room.*

LEFT: *Orderliness may be less a question of tidying everything away, than of making a place for the items you need, so that they are always ready to hand. Here a cutlery box and flowerpot hold the tools of an artist's trade.*

Comfortable Living

To arrange a home just as we would like it is to achieve a balance between ergonomics, whereby our surroundings work well according to our needs, and style, whereby they satisfy us visually. Getting the basic design right to begin with is, of course, crucial. But once the practical fittings are installed, your work has only just begun. Then it is time to add all the small, individual touches that make the place comfortable and personalize it according to your own sense of style. A decorative frieze, an inviting chair, a well-placed lamp, a wall hung with assorted pictures, are among the things that turn it into a home. And don't forget your lighting. Light draws us to an extent that we are not even aware of.

Lighting

The source of warmth and life, security and comfort, lighting is fundamentally important to us emotionally as well as in terms of physical convenience. Supplies of both daylight and artificial light dictate when we wake and sleep, and can affect our moods and our behavior.

LEFT: *A warm atmosphere is created by diffused uplighting from wall and shelf lights, firelight, and pools of light from small side-lamps.*

RIGHT: *The star motifs on the lampshade add dramatic focus to the corner of a room.*

Letting in the Light

In the past, glassmaking was highly expensive and large windows could only be enjoyed by the wealthy, but the twentieth-century invention of plate glass has made the luxury of interiors flooded with daylight widely available. Today we are far more conscious of the benefits of natural light than our predecessors, and opening up interiors with extra windows is a significant design aspect in building conversions. The advent of the well-designed, non-leak skylight has meant that countless windowless attics have been pressed into good use.

The oriental science of feng shui lays great emphasis on the aspect of a building – with good reason, since the direction a building faces decrees the amount and quality of daylight it receives. Rooms that benefit especially from natural light are the kitchen and the study or home office, where daytime activity is pivotal. Desks and work surfaces should be situated by windows, to let in light while avoiding self-cast shadows and glare caused by reflections.

BELOW: Skylight windows set into a sloping roof transform a dark attic into office space, the built-in work surface utilizing the supply of daylight.

LEFT: *If a bathroom window is overlooked, you need to make it impossible to see in from outside, while still allowing maximum light to enter. Instead of sheer curtains, why not try a semi-opaque blind or attractive frosted glass. A vase of fresh or dried flowers acts as a screen.*

LEFT: *Attic rooms, with their sloping walls under the eaves, make delightful bedrooms, especially for children, but the problem is often the lack of daylight. In this case the solution was a large skylight window set into the roof, softened by the folds of a lace curtain.*

LEFT: *Natural light is directed with the precision of floodlights to illuminate the dining room from the side, so that the transparent glass table and perspex chairs seem almost to float in light. Ceiling spotlights can be adjusted to focus on the shelves or on the table at mealtimes, or both.*

Screening the Light

Traditional buildings in hot countries are designed with small windows to keep rooms cool and shady; in contemporary buildings with picture windows, the alternative is to use roller or Venetian blinds, pulled partly or wholly down over windows, to shade interiors. Natural light still filters through, but rooms are kept refreshingly cool, and light-sensitive furnishings are protected.

Blinds are also a good solution for bedrooms and bathrooms, where privacy is as much of a priority as letting in the daylight, and have the added advantage of saving space in a small room. (To block out intrusive daylight completely, lightproof blackout fabric can be used.) If you hanker for a more romantic look, semi-transparent curtains provide privacy in a more traditional form.

RIGHT: Morning light in the bedroom is great when you wake up, but preferably without heat and glare, and not leaving you in full view of your neighbors! Classically pretty curtains in muslin, voile, or lace diffuse strong daylight and effectively maintain privacy.

ABOVE: The flat, tailored stretch of roller-blind fabric acquires pattern and texture with broad vertical stripes in strong color, crossing more roughly painted horizontal bands. Bold contemporary orange echoes warm sunlight, while screening out the heat of the day.

RIGHT: *A café curtain running across the bottom half of the window ensures privacy for breakfast in your dressing-gown, while allowing plenty of daylight to flood in from above. Unlined gingham lets some light through and looks fresh and cheerful.*

ABOVE: Plain cream roller blinds offer an excellent flat surface for embellishing with paintings, silk-screen prints, or, as here, decorative stampwork. The flying bird motif recalls the countryside outdoors, and the shape is given extra emphasis by natural illumination.

Reflecting the Light

Mirrors create their own virtual reality, giving the illusion of added dimensions. They also enhance daylight coming in through windows by reflecting the light back. This double illusion of increased light and space, together with the decorative effect of a fine frame, makes them a valuable and graceful addition to many interiors.

According to exponents of feng shui, mirrors are powerful because they draw energy towards them, thus helping to capture, intensify, or deflect forces of positive or negative energy. This is perhaps only another way of expressing the fact that a mirror hung at the end of a dark hall seems to open and brighten it; the effect is even stronger if you install a light over the glass. A mirror placed opposite the windows of a small room makes the room seem bigger.

When choosing a mirror make sure the surface gives you an undistorted image before you buy. In the past, when large sheets of mirror glass were hugely expensive, smaller ones were hung in groups to add to the effect of light and space, and this can still look good today. When candles or small lamps are placed in front of a mirror the light is redoubled.

ABOVE AND BELOW: Plain or carved frames for mirrors are greatly enhanced by decorative paint effects, especially gilding and antiqued silver.

ABOVE: Secondhand mirrors can be bought cheaply, and frames rejuvenated by painting.

LEFT: A well-proportioned decorative frame can be a work of art in itself.

OPPOSITE: The fine full-length mirror, strategically placed, adds light and elegance to a luxuriously spacious bathroom, while giving the room a double function as a dressing room.

Uplighters and Downlighters

Lighting is often neglected in home decorating, but it is too important to ignore. The single, central overhead light that illuminates so many rooms can kill relaxed intimacy at the flick of a switch. Today there is real variety in the lighting you can use and it is worth doing a little homework into how best to light your living space, for both function and atmosphere, before fittings are installed.

Uplighters and downlighters can help to emphasize a room's best features and downplay its weaknesses. Uplighters heighten a ceiling and help to flatten out a slope, and if set among plants will throw dramatic shadows on the walls. Downlighters help to keep attention away from a too-lofty ceiling, or, if recessed into the ceiling, can spotlight pictures or display shelves.

OPPOSITE: *Wall-mounted lights, throwing a subdued upward beam to bounce back off the ceiling, are an alternative to the central hanging light. A stenciled ivy pattern around this uplighter fitting is illuminated when the light is on, bringing out the fresh, leafy effect.*

LEFT: *Kitchens need to be both well lit for food preparation, and conducive to eating and hospitality. Here recessed downlighters throw effective light over work surfaces; the sink is under the window, for good natural light. Separately controlled lighting is needed for eating areas.*

347

Sidelighting

In a living area, a variety of lighting will almost certainly be needed for different activities and moods. Several light sources in a room have a softer and more relaxing effect than a single one, and are far more versatile.

Background lighting installations might be central pendant, spotlights, wallwashers, uplighters, or downlighters. Sidelights, table lamps, and task lights for specific working areas are also commonly used to add small washes of light to display ornaments, or for reading, writing, or sewing. Freestanding standard lamps serve similar purposes. The advantage of these lights is that they can be easily moved around. Try out the height and strength of lighting when positioning a light: the shade should hide fitting and bulb from the person seated, and needs to cast a downward beam strong enough for reading.

ABOVE: *Small candlestick lamps are cozy and space-saving. Paint effects to "age" a plain metal lampshade and wooden candlestick can be stunningly effective.*

RIGHT: *The pool of light cast by a table lamp beside a comfortable armchair makes an instantly inviting corner for reading and relaxing.*

LEFT: *The painted shade used with this modern, wrought-iron standard lamp casts downward light, except through the cutout shapes which throw starlights upward.*

Table Lamps

Apart from their functional aspect of illuminating specific activities, sidelights and table lamps add soft atmospheric background light. Several lamps fitted with low-wattage bulbs add a warm, cozy glow. Most lamps can have a dimmer fitted to the flex; if the light seems too bright and glaring, especially against a dark wall, try the effect of warm-colored bulbs or shades. The shape of the shade controls the spread of light: a conical shade gives a wide beam below the lamp, a cylindrical one funnels it into a narrow beam above and below, less suitable for reading.

Like candles and oil lamps in the past, sidelights and table lamps cast pools of light that define certain areas – comfortable seating for after-dinner conversation, for instance. Strategically placed lights can also create atmosphere by focusing on a particular decorative aspect: lamps set close to curtains draw attention to the fabric's texture and the shadows made by the folds, adding richness and dramatic emphasis.

In the bedroom, use well-shaded bedside lamps with easily reachable switches, and test that they are the right height for reading in bed. You will also need more functional background lighting for dressing.

ABOVE: *Although table lamps less usually take the form of uplighters, they can be a useful way of adding diffuse rather than direct light. You can define a seating area in a large room by setting an uplighter at either end of a sofa.*

OPPOSITE TOP AND OPPOSITE BOTTOM: *Lampstands and shades that are commercially available can be individualized by painting, appliquéing, or otherwise decorating your own. When choosing a base, remember that a heavy-bottomed vase or urn shape is less liable to tip over.*

ABOVE: *Decorated lampshades add an individual touch to your lighting. Stamped or stenciled motifs are especially effective on plain colored lampshades. The pattern should not be so heavy that it cuts out the light.*

351

Living by Candlelight

With all the sophisticated lighting equipment at our disposal, when we want to create an intimate ambience after dark there is still nothing to beat the oldest remedy of all – candles. Human beings are phototropic, meaning that we are drawn to light, and the flickering gleam of candlelight is uniquely attractive. Its soft glow is simultaneously dramatic and intimate, creating a unique atmosphere – no romantic dinner for two is complete without a central candle drawing the couple together.

It takes one-hundred and twenty candles to give the light of one 100-watt bulb, so living entirely by candlelight like our ancestors is hardly feasible; but the lighting of candles is a traditional and much-loved part of Christmas, Thanksgiving, and anniversary celebrations. Candles lit with a taper as family or friends gather around the dining table turn any evening meal into a special occasion, adding luster and sparkle to the table-settings; and the glow of candles on the mantelshelf adds romance to the hearthside.

ABOVE AND ABOVE RIGHT:
Hurricane lamps and
lanterns are a good idea if
you are eating outside or
with the windows open in
summer, when candles
sputtering in the wind can
be distracting. They also
protect the table from hot,
melted wax. Lanterns can
be hung outside on branches
or on lantern-holders stuck
in the ground.

RIGHT: The gentle play of
light from candles, mounted
in slender candlesticks over
dark oak paneling, is
timelessly attractive.

OPPOSITE: A dinner table-
setting in a large bay
window is lit by a regiment
of candles in assorted
holders around the
windowsill, adding light
and atmosphere without
using up table space.

LEFT: *High drama in a dinner setting entirely lit by candlelight. The stately central candelabra illuminates the table without interrupting the diners' line of vision, single candles glow at table level, and wall sconces light the edges of the room – all reflected back by the magnificent mirror.*

Candleholders

Rationally speaking, there is no need for candles in the power-driven, Western world – even during power cuts, you can light your way with a battery-charged flashlight. But if practicality were the only consideration, we would never bother with any of the graces of home decorating once the basic furnishings had been installed. The fact is that people are sustained by the need for variety, as well as by the essentials of life, and the way we live at home should allow for the expression of our changing moods.

Evocative and atmospheric, candles help to set the stage for life on a different plane. This is why candles are, if anything, more popular than ever, and why the holders we put them in are becoming more and more varied. There are elaborate single silver candlesticks and branched candlebras for the traditionalist, or starkly simple black metal holders for a minimalist's bedroom. The positioning of the right kind of candleholder within your decorative scheme can make all the difference.

ABOVE: A five-branched, brass candelabra casts a romantic glow on the table. It has been transformed to antique status with verdigris paint effects – and threaded with ivy for added glamor.

RIGHT: The ethereal glow of candlelight reflected in a mirror is richly atmospheric, offset by dark, textured walls.

LEFT: Plain white candles and white lilies are mirrored together in a still life composition perfected by the wide blue frame.

*ABOVE: Lustrous candles in antique silver holders
add opulence and brilliance to the formal beauty of
this mantelshelf arrangement.*

Storage

One of the big issues of contemporary living is how to be comfortably accommodated in a space that never seems big enough, and still find a place for everything. The solution lies in your storage arrangements. That – and controlling your accumulative instincts – is the heart of the matter.

LEFT: In this small kitchen, every inch of alcove space is used for cupboard shelving, wine rack, and food jars; dried herbs and spices hang nearby.

RIGHT: Shelving needn't be dull. Where did you put that paintbrush?

ABOVE: *A well-finished cupboard with molded plinth and cornice gets a new look with a chicken wire door and an interior coat of dark paint, excellent for displaying choice pieces of china.*

ABOVE RIGHT: *Utilize every corner of space – in this case literally, with a triangular corner cupboard which hides clutter inside while storing matching jars on top.*

Kitchen Cupboards

No room has more pressing need for storage than the kitchen. Along with sink, stove, fridge, and freezer, a place must be found for dried and fresh food, pans and cooking utensils, dishes and cutlery, cleaning things – all the paraphernalia of food preparation.

Do you want your storage units to display or conceal their contents? A kitchen with food storage jars and serving dishes on view is welcoming and practical, though shelves behind cupboard doors need less maintenance. Fitted cabinets or freestanding cupboards? Non-matching, free-standing storage is coming back into favor. Think vertically as well as horizontally – high cupboards can store the things you use less often.

One lifesaving guideline for planning kitchen and other household storage is to sort your possessions into three categories: essential, useful, and for occasional use only. This tells you how much you need to store, and how to prioritize.

LEFT: *This small larder cupboard, with a simple stenciled motif like fretwork, can stand on a work surface or be hung on a wall and is useful for keeping ingredients or condiments close at hand. Without an old-fashioned larder separate from the kitchen, allowance must be made for food that needs storing in cool, dark conditions.*

BELOW: *These fitted kitchen units have some display shelving, open and with glass doors, for plants and pretty china, while most items are hidden behind doors and in drawers. Much-used spoons and spatulas are kept to hand.*

RIGHT: *A rack for eggs and seasonings is kept ready to hand on the work surface. Keep a salt crock beside the cooker. Hang garlic and peppers in strings, or store in a terra-cotta jar.*

ABOVE: *Wooden plate-racks for drying and storing crockery have made a comeback. If you store your plates in a rack, try not to overcrowd it and sort the plates by size for an orderly effect. A stainless steel rack suits a modern, minimalist kitchen.*

RIGHT: *Open shelves look good in a rustic kitchen where food is stored in mixed earthenware crocks, glass jars, and bottles. A marble surface is a cool place to stand provisions. Fruit and vegetables can be stored in baskets under the work surface.*

Kitchen Racks and Shelves

Open storage suits today's more relaxed kitchens, where preparing food is a part of life to be shared with family and friends. While practicality is your first consideration, you want the kitchen to look good too. Storage jars of dried and bottled foodstuffs kept on open shelves are both highly accessible and visually attractive, reminiscent of the old-fashioned larder stocked with provisions.

Metal kitchen shelving in a Modernist loft performs the same function as the traditional hutch (dresser), storing and displaying dishes and plates, and acting as a sideboard for serving food. Make use of vertical space with wall-racks and rails for stacking and hanging utensils. Hooks, for hanging pots, jugs, mugs, and cups close to wherever they are needed, save surface space and are efficient time-savers, too. Do bear in mind that when everything is on show, orderliness is essential – and don't display items you never use; they will just gather dust.

ABOVE: In the kitchen, the home improvement enthusiast can go to town on painted shelving to store dishes and pots, and racks for hanging decorative dried flowers, herbs and spices, scented lavender bags, and dish towels. A carved apron enhances a plain cupboard.

LEFT: *Today's kitchen designers have brought built-in cupboards and shelving to state-of-the-art perfection tailored exactly to your needs and the space at your disposal. These cupboard doors have shelving inside and baskets slide out as drawers.*

RIGHT: *A stack of artfully stenciled hatboxes looks light and feminine, and makes excellent storage – not only for hats. Lateral thinking, the essence of clever storage, includes the way you fold things: roll towels and T-shirts to fit them into awkward spaces, for instance.*

Bedroom Storage

Your bedroom is your inner sanctum, and because it gets little through-traffic, it tends to be the place where you accumulate clothes, books, magazines, shoes . . . Yet clutter is the last thing you want in your private space, where an orderly atmosphere is needed to help you to sleep.

"Before you let anything into your life, you have to let something go" – the feng shui saying is only common sense. So before rushing off to buy a new wardrobe, take a good look at what it is to contain. Anything you can't remember when you last wore, or that you never felt comfortable in, will have to go. Now you can reward yourself with the prospect of new storage.

Freestanding or fitted wardrobes and drawers, trunks, chests, and baskets are useful and good-looking. Store shoes in drawers under the bed, or in hanging canvas caddies. With bedroom storage sorted, you can sleep easy.

ABOVE: A wooden shoe-rack tucks neatly under a rail of clothes in a wardrobe.

ABOVE RIGHT: A metal frame with tent top and curtains for the sides makes a pretty, practical, freestanding wardrobe.

RIGHT: Put jewelry and makeup in decorative boxes or baskets with lids, to keep the dressing table tidy.

BELOW: *A cupboard under the basin utilizes "dead" space for everything that needs to be hidden; the basin surround supplies a surface for toiletry essentials, with alcove shelving below.*

RIGHT: *A wooden, decorated box keeps spare soaps and sponges dry. Plunder the rest of the house for useful containers: a plastic bin with lid keeps things dry in a shower cubicle.*

OPPOSITE: *A stenciled cupboard is hung above the basin on one side, and a shelf on brackets on the other, neatly combining storage and display. Towels are at hand on a rack.*

Bathroom Storage

The bathroom is often the smallest room in the house, yet it is surprising how much there is to keep in it, especially for a family. At the very least you need shelf room by the basin for toothbrushes and shaving and washing things, and cupboard space for medicines and other essentials (turn out shelves regularly and throw away out-of-date medicines). Cleaning equipment also needs to be stashed away. In a small shower room, you might install a shelf above the showerhead; a corner cupboard or shelf takes up minimal space. The backs of doors come in handy to hang dressing-gowns, laundry bags, and canvas or plastic holders with multiple pockets. Under-used space above the toilet could hold shelves or bags on hooks.

In a larger bathroom, make sure the furniture you install won't be affected by a damp, steamy atmosphere. Use windowsills and alcove space to display visually attractive bottles, sponges, and brushes, and hide away the rest. Make use of containers from other rooms: baskets, enamel pails, even a colander where sponges can drain. Facecloths, and string bags holding children's bathtime toys, can drain from a row of small hooks. Some people like reading in the bath, but magazines have a marked tendency to accumulate – be ruthless in your tidying.

RIGHT: Toning stripes, checked binding and base, and sturdy tasseled rope ties turn a laundry bag into a stylish accessory, lined for heavy duty use and round-based for extra volume.

Laundry

Laundry is hardly a priority for most people planning a home, but it is worth giving some thought to it, since unwashed clothes hanging around the place are a distinct turn-off. Where are you going to store dirty linen: in the bedroom, or is there space in the bathroom? Your washing machine and dryer can be in the utility room if you have one, or in the bathroom or kitchen if not.

Washing powders and fabric conditioners kept on a shelf above or beside the machine keep the process streamlined. Do you have a clothes-horse or airer for drying washing? If you can hold on to a routine of sorting and folding washing as soon as it's dry – keep ironing separate and try not to let it become mountainous – then storing it is no problem.

ABOVE: A foldaway canvas laundry bag on a plain wooden frame looks neat and functional in a bathroom.

ABOVE RIGHT: Wicker is ideal for laundry – strong, flexible, aerated but hiding the contents. Line it with a removable cotton bag that can be emptied on washday.

RIGHT: Freshly ironed linen hung to air on a clothes-horse, makes a virtue out of necessity. An old-fashioned airer on a hoist, in the kitchen or bathroom, is a boon if you are short of space.

RIGHT: *A bureau with hinged lid and pigeonholes is invaluable for filing household papers and stationery. Drawers beneath can be used to file more papers and magazines. The doors for the shelves have been fitted with chicken wire for a contemporary look.*

RIGHT: *Stenciled wooden stands for stationery and mail are a neat, functional, and decorative solution to the infuriating problem of papers strewn over a desk surface. Papers are stored tidily, yet are accessible and visible at a glance. Wire or wicker baskets give an alternative look.*

LEFT: A raised stand for a computer screen is both ergonomically sound and space-saving. Building a separate stand, or the whole desk, is a fine project for an amateur carpenter. Papers hung on a bulldog clip keep the desk uncluttered and remind you of schedules or pressing jobs.

Organizing Work and Hobbies

Whatever happened to all those prophecies about the paperless office? Even those who don't work at home need a corner to do the household bills and file away letters, bills, receipts, and multifarious papers that mount up alarmingly. At the same time, more people are working from home each year and making their "workstation" from the kitchen table, a board set on trestles in the attic, a desk in the living room, or a table in the spare bedroom.

Depending on what you do, the first priority is clearly to install the essential equipment: a computer and usually a printer, along with phone and fax are top of most people's lists. Do you have enough electric and telephone sockets? Furniture layout should be decided before these are installed.

RIGHT: *Everything in its proper place: folding doors reveal a carpenter's haven, neatly laid out with tools and workbench under the stairs.*

Papers needn't necessarily be stored in a conventional filing cabinet; you can fit a trunk or deep-drawered desk with hanging files, or have a hanging filing system fitted behind hitch (dresser) doors, or stack color-coded files in baskets or boxes. Hoarders of books should invest in good-quality shelves that won't bow in the middle.

A desk or office equipment in the bedroom or living room can be an unwelcome reminder of work not done: hide it behind a folding screen or plantstand. Work-surface space can be increased by a cart (trolley) whose bottom shelf can hold files or reference magazines. Add a place for a sound deck if you like working to music.

"Provide places for all your things, so that you may know where to find them at any time, day or night." Those wise words from Mother Ann, founder of the Shakers in the 1770s, have a special resonance today when so many people are short of time and space. It's just as annoying not to be able to find some garden or carpentry tool when you are fired up for a weekend project, as it is to have lost vital papers for work. We lose weeks and months out of our lives just hunting for things. So, try to reduce the volume by throwing out what you don't use, and then keep things together. You can have fun with containers – bags, boxes, pots, antique or oriental chests or suitcases are all grist to the storage mill.

LEFT: Save sewing, embroidery, and knitting materials and equipment from spreading all over the sitting room with a sturdy homemade workbag, hung up when not in use.

375

RIGHT: Neatly folded clean linen and blankets look enticing on display in the shelves of a carved linen press, rejuvenated with a coat of distressed paint and chicken wire doors.

Storage Cupboards

The storage cupboards you choose will depend on your decorating style: pretty linen presses from France, Germany, and Hungary are perfect for country style, while heavy English wardrobes and side-cupboards suit the traditionalist. A modernist living area demands the functional simplicity of boxlike cabinets with minimal handles. A carved piece from India or Indonesia adds dramatic presence to a modern interior, or can be combined with other ethnic furniture and hangings for a more exotic effect.

When shopping for cupboards measure your space first and take your tape-measure with you. Go for the biggest piece you can accommodate but do take into account the size of your door frames, to avoid it getting stuck halfway in!

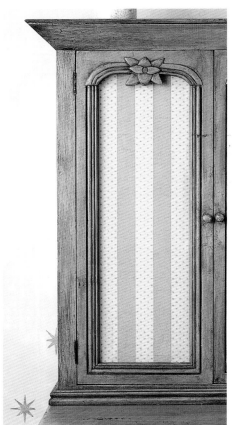

ABOVE: Cupboards and wardrobes are prime candidates for cheap, effective paint treatments. Fitted curtains in the doors look fresh and tempting, and keep out the dust. For this kitchen cupboard, traditional voile is sewn in narrow pleats for a neat, feminine look.

ABOVE RIGHT AND RIGHT: A cupboard can be dressed in various curtain styles. The simplest (top) uses a medium-weight cotton, stretched over the opening on fixed rods. Or, use a printed voile (bottom) for a bedroom.

Storage Boxes

Boxes and chests are among the simplest of all storage units, and also the most ancient. Once they were made as portable luggage for nomads or merchants, or for wealthy travelers with valuable possessions. Carved coffers were used for storing clothes or linen, while the bride's dower or hope chest accompanied her to her husband's home after marriage. Small boxes, sometimes beautifully decorated and with security locks, held coins and jewelry.

Large coffers and chests are still tremendously versatile storage for books, bedding, or clothes folded away out of season, and double up as low tables in a living room or bedroom. Paint a plain pine chest, or hunt for a carved ethnic one, if it suits your style. Antique canvas or tin trunks and well-polished leather suitcases are much in vogue for use in the same way. Children's rooms can be made magically tidy in minutes by roomy toy boxes. Bedroom dressing tables look soothingly uncluttered once you acquire the habit of keeping jewelry, hair and manicure things, buttons and pins, sorted into ornamental boxes. Modernists equip their offices with stacked cardboard or metal boxes for files and stationery. Use rough rustic boxes, or beautifully made, oval Shaker ones, in different sizes, color-coded according to contents.

ABOVE: Papier-mâché boxes in delightfully fanciful shapes, with decorations to match, are fine projects to make and charming presents to give and receive. This ambitious hexagonal one with legs and elephant lid could be used to stash candy, sewing accessories, or bathroom things.

ABOVE RIGHT: Once upon a time, sailors used to paint their wooden chests with sailing ships and marine scenes to pass the time on voyage. Today we can indulge our decorative fancies on pine chests or tin trunks and boxes; this one has sea creatures swimming on a green background.

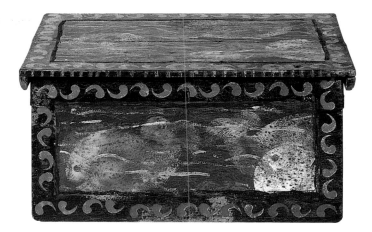

LEFT: *Again reminiscent of the sailor's chest, a blue, painted chest acquires a briny subterranean atmosphere with whales stamped over sides and lid, overlaid with the lines of waves, and a stenciled decorative border of wavy motifs.*

BELOW: *Even sewing on buttons could be a pleasure when sewing things are stored in a pretty workbox, whose padded lid is covered with a medieval flower tapestry. Cotton yarns have been used rather than wool, for a fresh, lustrous effect. Keep a lavender bag in the box to deter moths.*

Arranging a Room

Knowing the effect you want to create is halfway to achieving it. Having prepared the groundwork with color schemes and furniture, now you have the opportunity to add atmosphere and detail to your rooms by arranging the objects and images that give you most pleasure.

LEFT: *A cleverly organized kitchen has shelves containing most-used items in orderly array closest to hand, and a high shelf for display.*

RIGHT: *The well-arranged room has a place for scent, touch, color, and luxury.*

ABOVE: *For a modern variation on the eighteenth-century print rooms use either paper or painted ribbons, bows, cords, tassels or other trimmings, as here, to unify and frame a display of small images and objects. Today you can buy complete packs with trompe l'oeil frames and borders.*

Hanging Pictures and Prints

Framed pictures, mirrors, ceramics, and wall-hangings all add substance to your style. Framing and hanging can be a thoroughly enjoyable exercise, and offers plenty of scope to show off to greatest effect the things you treasure.

Have you chosen cool minimalism, a comfortably cluttered country look, or classic period style? Your images and frames will accentuate the look, whatever your preference. A collection of small prints, photographs, or paintings looks good arranged together on a single wall, in a stepped arrangement up a staircase wall, or surrounding a central doorway. While symmetrical groupings are always pleasing, a well-balanced asymmetrical display can be more intriguing.

ABOVE: *Small pictures, prints, and ceramics are grouped together for effect. To experiment without damaging the wall, decide on the overall arrangement, trace around individual images, and stick them in place with masking tape.*

OPPOSITE: *A stepped assembly of prints in frames of equal size, but given different paint treatments, gives a feeling of order. Note the equidistant gap between pictures – about half the width of the image is a guide.*

Framing

The type of frame you choose depends on your decorating style. An important picture demands an ornate frame to offset it, and plenty of wall space. A series of prints looks good in matching frames; a mixed collection of prints can be linked visually by similar mounts and frames. Contemporary photographs look best framed in plain black, chrome, or wood; old portraits are charming in oval mounts and frames.

Junk shops are full of old framed pictures which you can recycle to frame your own pictures. The simplest coordinating trick is to paint or stain several plain wooden frames with the same color.

ABOVE: Junk shop finds are excellent for experimenting with paint effects, and gilding and antiquing can effectively transform a molded frame. Framing is a real art, and specialty books can help with exact step-by-step techniques.

LEFT: A collection of old maps is put in similar dark frames as a visual link, and hung between two windows to give the grouping its own frame. The different sized pictures are cleverly arranged to emphasize their similarities.

ABOVE AND LEFT: *Burls and graining add individual texture to different wood veneers, enhanced by stains and varnishes to supply richness and depth. Ornamental penwork (left) adds color and decorative detail to plain wooden frames.*

FAR LEFT: *A series of botanical photographs is similarly mounted in matching frames, the written descriptions forming part of the composition. A confident, striking overall arrangement holds the group together on the wall.*

Displaying Collections

Collecting is an enjoyable way to employ the magpie in us, as well as to learn about the history and use of the objects in question. The pleasure is in the pursuit, and value is not necessarily an intrinsic part of it – you might collect corkscrews, or dolls, worth only a few pounds each, which acquire importance and special interest in numbers.

Displaying your collection calls other talents into use. The art of placement is about presenting things in a group with careful attention to detail, so that they make a well-balanced whole. Are they the kind of objects that look best on shelves, with lighting directed on them to focus attention? Or could they be hung on a wall? A collection of humble wooden spoons from all over the world – ornately carved, roughly hewn – looks wonderful on a wall painted azure blue or dusty Indian red. Valuable porcelain or delicate objects need to be protected as well as displayed; glass-fronted cabinets, fitted shelves in an alcove, and stepped Japanese cupboards are among the options.

Maybe you would like your collection to be a movable feast: left too long in the same place those treasured items may be ignored and gather dust. Or store your collection in woven baskets or boxes, arranged in a row or stack. When arranging your collection, think about how lighting could focus on it and accentuate its features.

BELOW: A partitioned shelving system of wood or even cardboard, if its load is light, can be hung on the wall to hold a display of decorative objects.

BELOW RIGHT: Modest earthenware plates become beautiful in their glass-fronted cupboard whose diamond panes tone with the blue interior.

OPPOSITE: The art of placement is demonstrated by a collection of hats hung on a landing wall; more can be added above the door and at the base of the wall. In the bedroom, a group of matching leather suitcases, neatly tiered atop the wardrobe, is visually arresting and a practical storage solution.

Arranging Cushions

Cushions must be one of the oldest forms of upholstery, softening and adding comfort to hard seats or even the floor. These invaluable extras help to define and refine your decorating style, adding color and luxury, and the atmospheric detail that lifts a room and makes it special.

For a country house look, use flowered prints, paisleys, brocades, and tapestries, with lots of braids and tassels for trimmings. Simple stripes and checks in toning colors look good with patterns or, in a modern room, with plain upholstery. If the look is right you can use extravagant silks and velvets, in dramatic splashes of color. Buttons add tailored detail, contrasting ties look feminine, and round bolsters with buttons or tassels give a classic touch.

OPPOSITE: The revival of traditional ribbonwork is well suited to a country-style living room or bedroom. Try overlapping stripes on a square cushion, or in bands around a bolster.

RIGHT: A bevy of cushions in different tartans looks dashing on a tartan throw over a comfortable chair. Cord piping, tassels, braids, and ribbons add to the smart, tailored look. Checked and plain tweeds also accessorize well.

ABOVE RIGHT: Cushions are a splendid showcase for your sewing, embroidery, or silk-painting skills. This jewel-colored painted design looks great with matching plain silk cushions against dark upholstery.

RIGHT: Sumptuous tapestry, embroidery, and bargello work add a touch of opulence as well as rich color and pattern in a traditional setting. A handsome matching braid acts as frame to finish your handiwork.

LEFT: This room owes its atmosphere to successful arrangement. The bold canvas above the sofa, pleasing alcove decoration, and strikingly arranged mantelshelf and flowers, plus the bright contrasting cushions, marry well with the comfortable placing of sofas and chairs.

LEFT: *A charming posy compliments this chic breakfast tray, with matching china and fun newspaper wrapping.*

OPPOSITE: *Superb red amaryllis emerge dramatically from bulbs anchored among small and large pebbles in a square, glass container.*

RIGHT: *A blue-and-white bowl is packed with purple, blue, and white spring flowers and senecio foliage – ideal for the table or windowsill.*

ABOVE: Graceful sprays of lilies are held in place by transparent glass marbles inside a square, glass container.

Flower Arrangement

Flowers are intensely appealing to the senses, lifting our spirits with their delicate scents and textures and vivid colors. There is something moving about their fragile impermanence, and they add life and beauty to any room.

Yet although flowers themselves will never go out of fashion, the art of arranging them has been revolutionized to adapt to modern living. Today's simple, spontaneous arrangements allow us to appreciate flowers for themselves, rather than the arranger's art; and garden flowers, with their imperfections, are as much prized as flawless hothouse blooms. Stately floral structures are replaced by sheafs of daffodils or iris in simple glass containers.

Whatever your style and preference, decide first where to put your display. Do you want the flower colors to contrast with the room's color scheme or to blend in with it? A complementary dash of scarlet looks stunning in a green room, while a mixture of pink and red flowers could echo country chintzes in similar hues. What container to use? A shallow bowl will spread your arrangement more widely, a tall square or cylindrical shape holds stems upright.

ABOVE: Sunny orange and white gerbera are casually tied with coarse string and stood in a terra-cotta pot for a summery, modern look.

ABOVE: Hot-hued pink, red, and orange flowers contrast with the blue and white jug in this delightful, country-style display. The near-central peony is its focus, with roses arranged around it and lilies, stocks, columbine, and glory lilies fanning out to add height and shape.

Chicken wire or floral foam inside the vase helps to anchor stems. In a mixed arrangement, the biggest blooms are best in the center, with smaller sprays graduating outward. Add twigs, leaves, and buds to vary the outline. An odd rather than even number of blooms somehow creates a more informal effect.

A shallow display is best for table-settings, to prevent guests from having to duck around a jungle of foliage to speak to each other. A basket filled with blowzy garden roses, their stems freshened by presoaked floral foam hidden under moss, looks divinely rustic for a summer supper. Mix sprigs of sweet herbs – parsley, coriander, or rosemary – with flowers for added fragrance.

Today's arrangements often show the influence of China and Japan, where just one or two blooms are arranged in a simple, stylized display. A Western adaptation of oriental restraint is to have a repeat pattern of a single bloom in a small vase or glass, each positioned at the same angle, along the center of a table or across a mantelpiece.

ABOVE: *Summer meals outside on patio or terrace can combine a massed array of container plants at their peak with the table-setting. Bright geraniums, impatiens, auricula, and others vie for attention with bowls of succulent fruits of the season.*

RIGHT: *Rustic, striped pots of miniature yellow roses look charming and fresh in a curlicued wrought-iron holder hung on a wall in the bathroom.*

ABOVE: *A statuesque display of foliage in a tall holder can transport the magical freshness of spring into a sunny interior. Set in a decorative plantstand beside the table in a wide bay window, these oak branches with their young green leaves are graceful and theatrical.*

Indoor Plants

Container plants add life and freshness even to a dark interior, and for many city-dwellers without a garden they supply much-needed contact with growing, living things.

Many and various tropical plants will thrive in heated rooms, so long as you look after them properly. Group them together for a natural, jungly look; spotlit from behind, their shadows add dramatic presence. Evergreen foliage can be supplemented by containers of spring and summer flowers, which add color and scent and last far longer than cut flowers.

Make sure furniture surfaces are protected from spills when you water plants, and don't keep plants on a windowsill above a radiator – it will leave them parched. Indoor plants are often killed by kindness through overwatering, so follow growing instructions. If you lack green fingers, a collection of tiny pots of cacti is surprisingly decorative!

RIGHT: Massed bulbs of miniature narcissi, kept damp by sphagnum moss lining a wire basket, are a thrilling herald of spring.

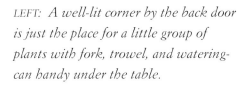

LEFT: *A well-lit corner by the back door is just the place for a little group of plants with fork, trowel, and watering-can handy under the table.*

ABOVE: *Ferns love shade and humidity, and are happiest away from direct sun in a corner of a steamy bathroom, or close to the sink in a kitchen.*

LEFT: *White flowers and variegated ivy look charming in a decorated wooden planter or terra-cotta pots.*

Patios and Terraces

It's amazing how time-consuming – and rewarding – gardening in a small outdoor space can be. A sunny rooftop, shady semi-basement plot, or tiny backyard effectively becomes an extra room which you can arrange as you like, with architectural features, furniture, permanent foliage, and containers full of plants. Movable containers add flexibility to your arrangement, so that you can bring shape, texture, and color to wherever they are needed.

Style is a priority. Do you like a wild, jungly look? Walls and trellises with lots of climbing and creeping plants provide plenty of foliage with relatively little maintenance. The meditative calm of a Japanese arrangement? This demands

RIGHT: *Inexpensive terra-cotta pots can be given a bright paint treatment before they are planted up for patio or interior use. Use ordinary latex (emulsion) paint with acrylic varnish as a sealant; these sunflowers are cut out from wrapping paper and glued in place.*

stringent structural design and restraint in the plants you introduce. Traditional cottage-garden charm? Bright herbaceous-border perennials and annuals will attract butterflies and bees even in the center of town.

Terra-cotta, concrete, wood, plastic, and metal containers can be customized with paint effects. Where are you going to put your pots, and what will you be planting? Terra-cotta is stunning planted with red and orange plants, for instance, while silvery foliage looks good in a metallic container. Blues, pinks, and grays are misty and subtle in effect; purple with white is smart and formal. Aromatic and edible salad herbs are both attractive and useful. Overplant rather than underplant for a generous effect, keep your trowel and watering-can to hand, and feed your plants regularly to reap your visual reward.

BELOW LEFT: A square wooden container with beveled corner posts, is a neat foil for decoratively clipped box or other types of topiary.

BELOW RIGHT: Contrasting feathery pinnate and palmate foliage in variegated and plain greens looks good in metal or terra-cotta containers.

LEFT: *Careful planning, structure, and planting have turned a tiny patio into an enchanting outdoor room for summer entertaining. The decorative trellis and pots on the wall add privacy, the bench and urn are framed by lush planting with elegant white flowers, and the round table maximizes the small space.*

Children's Rooms

Nestbuilding is only natural, and the prospect of a new addition to the family is apt to send parents-to-be into a fever of decorating. When embarking on this, though, remember that babies soon grow into toddlers, then they're off to school, and before you know it your babies are into their teens . . .

LEFT: *This cheerful and practical room is well designed to grow up with its occupant. The built-in desk allows plenty of room for play or study, with storage below.*

RIGHT: *A child's room needs to have space for his or her best friends as well.*

RIGHT: *Friendly teddy needlepoint pictures are a nice project while you await the new arrival . . .*

FAR RIGHT: *A crib with a detachable side is big enough to turn into a toddler's first bed. A bedside rug is foot-friendly and protects fitted carpets.*

RIGHT: *For safety, choose furniture with no sharp edges and which can't be knocked over.*

The Nursery

Masses of furniture isn't essential in a room for a baby or toddler. Your basic nursery necessities are a crib; cupboard and shelves for diapers, clothes, and toys; a laundry bag or basket; lighting that includes a nightlight; curtains or blinds to screen daylight; and comfortable seating for parents. If you can, allow floor-space for a playpen and toys – the floor should be smooth, splinter-free and, like everything else in the room, washable. Choose a simple color scheme with enough color and pattern to be stimulating. Babies enjoy having interesting objects and shapes to look at, so add hanging mobiles and pictures.

Miniature furniture is very seductive and small children love having their own things, but remember that they quickly grow out of cribs and miniature chairs.

ABOVE: A cheerful rug and adaptable, easy-to-assemble shelving unit with painted drawers are quick budget solutions for the nursery.

Decorating the Walls

Painting the walls is the quickest way to transform a child's bedroom. Tempting as it is to stick to traditional pastels early on, bright primary colors are stimulating – children most often choose red as their favorite color! Do involve older children in decisions about decorating – they often have strong views and it can be a good early lesson in learning how to keep to a budget as well.

For a bright, modern look, paint the walls in kaleidoscopic colors: one purple, another yellow, a third blue, and the next red, with beanbags, bedcovers, and curtains in corresponding colors to pull it all together. Or choose a decorating theme: a nautical look is popular, or follow a craze for a favorite animal. If an all-over patterned wallpaper would be overdoing it, you could paper just the wall beside the bed. Alternatively, a paper or stenciled frieze could reflect the theme, just below the ceiling, or lower down like a chair rail. The frieze can be repainted or papered when teenage tastes take over. For children into computer technology, a high tech black-and-white theme, with a bright red or other primary bedcover, can be strong and stylish.

RIGHT: Another stencil design, this time used all over the walls above the chair rail, takes appealing giraffes as the main motif, with fluttering dragonflies adding to the more formal pattern of the pairs of animals.

FAR RIGHT: A charming way of decorating a child's room is to stencil a broad frieze of animals and leaves around the walls at the child's eye level, to be enjoyed from one's pillow when waking or going to sleep.

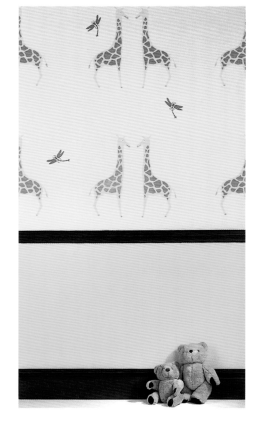

Curtains for Kids

Practically every designer worth their salt produces a range of children's designs these days, so there is a wonderful selection of textiles to choose from. Or, if you have time, you can embellish your own, with fanciful trimmings and decorative additions, with a little help from the kids.

Bright candy-stripes, ginghams, and checks are charming for the nursery; polka dots, with trimmings of toning fabrics with smaller dots, are bold and versatile. In a drafty room quilted curtains are pretty and cozy in winter, as are blankets hung on straps for a more tailored look. Whatever fabric you choose, make sure it is washable and flameproof.

BELOW: Fresh Madras cotton and gingham curtains, pinned back, have acquired a jolly trim of enormous petals along the bottom. The green-and-yellow fabrics tone with the paintwork, as well as with the dinosaurs which have taken joint possession of the room.

RIGHT: Bright blue curtains with yellow polka dots have detachable giant padded numbers in contrasting fabrics, which can be moved around and stuck back on with hook-and-loop fastening. Clever and entertaining, they turn early arithmetic lessons into fun.

LEFT: *When these curtains are drawn at night they reveal bands of lions, tigers, crocodiles, and birds trooping cheerfully across the windows, their vivid colors matching the abstract frieze along the walls. The horizontal stripes accentuate the width of the windows.*

LEFT: *A high platform bed with a neat ladder for access makes bedtime an enticing prospect, and is a sensible solution when space is short. This leaves room underneath for a cozy den with a storage chest and curtains to hide toys and clutter, while floor-space is freed up for playing.*

411

RIGHT: *The more enticing a container is, the more likely it is to be used. Painted wooden boxes can store pencils, marbles, paperclips, coins, and other small treasures.*

ABOVE: *A toy box becomes a treasure-chest with paper horses, created with a stencil template, stuck down with glue and varnished.*

RIGHT: *A roomy box stashes away toys in seconds. This one, covered with fabric, has acquired its jolly polka dots through being stamped with a round sponge, saturated in non-absorbent, acrylic paint.*

Children's Storage

The need for storage is ever-increasing as children grow older, and there should always be enough space to stow things away, to provide the incentive for tidying up. A chest with drawers or a small wardrobe for clothes, shelves for books and toys, and a toy-chest, are basic essentials. Space beneath beds can be used for drawers on casters.

Children love suitcases, and packing things away in cardboard or canvas cases stacked in tiers can be fun. A built-in corner cupboard with curtains around it can hide boxes underneath.

As kids grow so do their hobbies: skates and other sports equipment can be hung on pegrails. An electric train circuit mounted on hardboard can be stood on its side or even hoisted to the ceiling with a rope and pulley. Desk space for homework is essential, with electric circuits tucked away close by for the computer age.

ABOVE: A simple, sturdy child's desk has sunken compartments to keep pens and pencils from rolling off and getting lost.

LEFT: Drawings, photos, and paintings can be pinned onto a cork notice-board. A wall-mounted blackboard is also a good idea, for spelling practice and messages.

Screens and Disguising

Practical solutions to decorating dilemmas often involve the art of illusion. Screening a work area, dividing a room, hiding or disguising functional equipment behind a handsome facade, can seem problematic but may be simply arranged with a folding screen, ingenuity, and imagination.

LEFT: *Folding screens, whose Moorish design is echoed by the hanging lanterns, elegantly hide bedroom and office in a one-room living area.*

RIGHT: *Plain, functional furniture is magically disguised by decorative gilding and paintwork.*

Room Screens

Living in modern open-plan houses and loft apartments, we are returning in an odd way to the past, when rooms were not divided according to function and when people washed in bedrooms, bathed in the kitchen, and ate in the hall or living room. Folding portable screens were often used to divide rooms, provide privacy, or serve as draft excluders behind fireside chairs.

Screens were also traditionally used in oriental interiors; in China a painted or lacquered scene added attraction to a simple room. To separate different living areas the Japanese use paper and bamboo screens which can be slid sideways or folded back against the wall when not in use.

Not so long ago, antique Victorian and Edwardian scrap screens covered with nostalgic decoupage were all the rage. Today the trend is for a simpler look using fabric panels, or paper, or woven wicker panels to go with popular neutral colors.

ABOVE: A woven latticework of broad ribbons, in subtle color combinations, has been ingeniously used to fill the panels of a folding screen with a simple wooden frame.

RIGHT: A zany modern patchwork of paperboard (card), roughly painted in similar-toned contemporary colors and cut into almost identical rectangles, is held together with neat metal links.

OPPOSITE: Charmingly stylized stencil designs of lilies in a pot, above a garden of daisies, decorate an elegant screen for a traditional or country-style room.

LEFT: *A classic country look, especially good with dark oak furniture, this delightful needlepoint picture depicting the fable of the fox and the crow, echoes the fine detail of medieval embroideries.*

ABOVE: *Create an old-fashioned screen with nostalgic Victorian cutouts glued to the surface and coated with yellow, satin varnish.*

Small Screens

Small screens are the conventional way to fill an empty fireplace which looks bleak and uninviting when left unlit in summer; they can also hide a television set or other modern technology whose presence jars in a traditionally decorated room. And they offer an excellent opportunity for you to show off your skills at embroidery, needlepoint, quilting, or silk-painting.

Secondhand fire screens can often be picked up for next to nothing in junk shops and you can recycle the structure, which is essentially a picture frame on a stand, with your own handiwork. Old-fashioned samplers, and fragments of beautiful antique textiles trimmed to the size of the frame, also look good in this context, drawing your eye to focus on its decorative detail.

Dividing Rooms

In the era of one-room apartments, with space at a premium, we can borrow lessons in space management from the Japanese, who rigorously divide and define household zones with sliding rice-paper walls which can be opened up at other times to maximize a small living area. In the same way, we need our living space to be adaptable and versatile, and to have the means to close off a kitchen, bedroom, or office at one time, and open it up again later.

Folding screens are one solution; sliding doors that let the light through are another. In many English Victorian houses large dividing doors were hung between the front parlor, for special occasions, and the back room for everyday use, and these are still handsome and practical. Curtains draped back with decorative ties can be used in the same way. In an open-plan apartment curtains can close off a bedroom space when guests are invited.

A stylish way to divide a living space between dining room and living room, for instance, is to hang a bamboo blind from the ceiling, so that light still filters through. Architects sometimes suspend or stand a half-wall, open above and below, so that zones are controlled while the overall effect is of open space. Another structural solution between kitchen and dining room, say, or for a bedroom with adjoining bathroom, is to borrow from oriental buildings a "broken" half-wall which stops short of the ceiling, with inset square holes that act as shelves for glass bottles and ornaments.

A well-thought-out lighting system can also be an effective room divider. In an open-plan kitchen and dining area, lighting dimmed over kitchen surfaces and focusing down on the dining table during meals acts like a screen or dividing door. A bead curtain across a doorway between kitchen and dining room is contemporary, cheerful, and cheap.

LEFT: *Draped curtains between a large, high living room and a conservatory extension can open up or divide the two areas, and act as a handsome frame for the view to the garden through picture windows. They can be closed for warmth in winter and to screen dazzling sunlight in summer.*

421

SCREENS AND DISGUISING

RIGHT: A battered tallboy has been "tartaned up" with colored latex (emulsion) paints and varnish sealer. Or leave the tallboy plain and tartan just the knobs!

ABOVE: Redecorate an old cupboard with the child's play technique of potato stamping on the inner panels and drawer front. A repeat pattern of diamonds and stripes in terra-cotta is stamped on a yellow ocher base.

Disguising Old Furniture

With your new apartment you inherited an old sideboard or bedside cabinet. It looks terrible, but you do use it, and getting rid of old furniture is almost as troublesome as finding a replacement. Seriously, now, wouldn't it be better to disguise its defects with some nifty paintwork?

These relatively small projects can be tackled in limited space over a weekend, and a decorative finish can really transform a reject, emphasizing its strong points while hiding weak ones. Heavy wardrobes can "shrink" visually under a distressed paint treatment in discreet colors that blend with the wall. Odd kitchen chairs can be linked by a painted color scheme or sponged design. A hutch (dresser) with a pretty stencil pattern on the doors becomes a pleasure to use. Try to match the visuals with the shape of the piece – joky stripes and checks with chunky utility-type cupboards, flat-painted folk designs for a carved hutch (dresser). Trays and tabletops respond well to geometric stenciling or lining.

BELOW: Colorful decoupage shapes cut from magazines add pattern and texture to a sideboard's door panels.

Party Style

Party time: time to pull out all the stops – the best china, polished silver, glowing candles, stunning flower arrangements, the lot. You are inviting people to celebrate, and you want everybody to enjoy themselves. To make an occasion truly special you need to stage-manage the preparation.

LEFT: *The formal symmetry of an opulent table-setting in gold, silver, green, and white is relieved by trailing fronds of ivy, softening the arrangement.*

RIGHT: *Make a silvery papier mâché dish for celebrations, complete with crown motif.*

ABOVE: *Keep a special scarlet window blind to hang at Christmastime, stamped or stenciled with golden stars.*

RIGHT: *A flowing staircase garland of pine is loaded with colorful ribbons and aromatic dried fruit, spices, and herbs.*

RIGHT: *This fine composition exploits the variety of evergreen leaf shapes and textures in a winter garden, the holly berries adding the traditional touch of scarlet for Christmas.*

Christmas Dressing

Time permitting, preparing for Christmas is at the heart of the celebrations. The theme you choose for the decorations will need to harmonize with the basic decor. Scandinavian style favors simplicity – fresh pine boughs adorned with candles, cookies cut in festive shapes, and red ribbons; wreaths of woven juniper; bowls of nuts and fruit. For a country or traditional look, festoon rooms and hallways with rich garlands of evergreens, fir-cones, dried flowers, and ribbons. In a modern room, use natural-looking aromatic bunches and parcels of spices and herbs – cinnamon, rosemary, lavender – on a sculptural arrangement of bare branches.

TOP: *Modeling material is rolled, cut into decorative shapes, and baked. Once cool, the shapes are sprayed with metallic paint; plastic jewels and gold cord are stuck on with glue.*

ABOVE: *This delicate, heart-shaped wreath is entwined with artificial leaves and dried flowers scented with rose oil.*

The Hearthside

Firelight casting a flickering glow over sparkling tinsel, evergreen leaves, and scarlet berries is an indelible childhood memory, and unlike others we can repeat it every year. The hearth has symbolized warmth, welcome, home, and hospitality since ancient times, and becomes the natural focus for festivities at Christmas.

As a variation on traditional red candles in silver candlesticks on the mantelshelf, plant church candles in gilded flowerpots filled with gilded nuts and stand them in a row, or arrange a bundle of twigs in a silver pail lit by a glowing veil of tiny lights. Arrange masses of holly and trailing ivy around the fireplace, and highlight leafy swags with an edging of gold paint. Sprinkle swags of evergreen with miniature drawstring bags in rich velvets and silks. A round or triangular moss tree in a pot is simply sculptural, while stately amaryllis adds an elegant splash of red.

ABOVE RIGHT: A centerpiece of candles, set in a base of fresh and dried fruit and flowers, nuts in small terra-cotta pots, fir-cones and aromatic lavender, creates a glowing, festive atmosphere.

RIGHT: A harmonious mantelscape of white and gold candles and cards decorated with gilded stamps creates a calm and tranquil look.

OPPOSITE: Poinsettia, Chinese lanterns, variegated holly, and mistletoe are woven with lacy twigs into a handsome symmetrical swag over the blazing hearth.

Easter Colors

Easter and spring come together, bringing the first flowers and early leaves of the year. This is the time of freshness and promise, symbolized by eggs that herald new life.

Easter is a lovely time of year to celebrate, especially with children to relish chocolate eggs of every shape and size: hide them in different rooms, or all around the garden, with clues written on parchment-type paper. Children also love decorating wooden or real (hardboiled!) eggs. Boil eggs rubbed with vinegar then wrapped in onionskins for a tie-dye effect; paint eggs with faces or traditional folk designs and pile them in bowls or baskets on a breakfast table (the traditional Easter feast).

Fluffy bunnies and yellow chicks are closely associated with Easter, and can be added to your central arrangements. So can delicate spring flowers: pale yellow primroses, bright primula, and delicate violets look enchanting in terra-cotta pots or wire containers lined with moss, as do smaller bulbs – grape hyacinths, blue scilla, miniature narcissi – or delicate wood anemones and woodruff. For bigger arrangements, branches of hazel catkins, pussy willow, and burgeoning chestnut buds bring spring over the threshold.

OPPOSITE: Long sashes of cream damask and yellow ribbons divide a round table for an elegant, formal Easter breakfast setting. A clutch of hens' and quails' eggs sits in the central nest, surrounded by delicate molded creamware, organdie place mats, and napkins tied with ribbons.

RIGHT: Eggs painted in brilliant jewel-like blues and purples are stamped with a turquoise and gold flower motif. The colors and design match the simple blue and yellow motifs of Easter chicks, eggs, and flowers stamped in paint on the plates and white cotton tablecloth.

ABOVE: Bright yellow flowers – miniature narcissi, dried goldenrod, and dyed alartum – are woven around the handle and rim of a wicker flower-basket to give a wreath-like effect. The basket is packed with scrap paper and covered with a bed of moss for nestling quails' eggs.

FABRIC CARE

To make your soft furnishings last longer and look better, try to handle them as little as possible. Most curtains and blinds will fade eventually, but you can delay the process by always drawing them back or up during the day unless, such as with sheer curtains, they are specifically designed to remain drawn or down. Spray on fabric protectors can be used on cushions and upholstery to produce a water-repellent silicon finish. This gives you time to wipe up any spilled liquid before it soaks in and stains. Soft furnishings are often soiled by household dust, so use a low-suction setting on your vacuum cleaner and clean regularly to prevent build up.

Dealing with small stains

Small stains can be dealt with on the spot. There are commercial brands of stain removers that work remarkably well on grease, wine, and coffee, for example. Blot away as much of the stain as possible first and test the stain remover on a leftover scrap of fabric or an unobtrusive corner. Avoid using water on silk or wool as it can cause discoloration and shrinkage. If you prick your finger while sewing soft furnishings, there is a quick way to remove spots of blood: simply moisten a length of cotton sewing thread with saliva and rub it against the spot until it is no longer visible.

Cleaning

Always follow the manufacturer's recommendations when cleaning fabrics. Dry cleaning is the best option for blinds and all but the simplest of curtains and, if possible, you should get them cleaned professionally rather than using proprietary sprays. Some companies will come and clean curtains and blinds on site and rehang them for you. You can wash simple, unlined curtains, but remember that many fabrics will shrink, especially those made from natural fibers. Check if the fabric can be machine washed, if the colors will run and if it will shrink during washing. If the fabric is not pre-shrunk, find out what the shrinkage percentage is and allow for this when estimating the amount you need. You must then prewash the fabric before making up. However, bear in mind that some fabrics will always shrink a little when washed. Make sure you leave an adequate hem that can be let down if necessary. Only wash blinds if the fabric is pre-shrunk and you are certain it will not shrink any more. Remove any brass rings, cording, and dowel rods first.

Never wash interlined curtains and only wash lined curtains when the lining is detachable. The lining fabric and main fabric may shrink by different amounts and the curtains lose body and finish.

When choosing fabrics for other soft furnishings, consider how the item is to be cleaned. Decide if you will need to wash the finished piece regularly, such as a tablecloth, and choose fabric accordingly. Prewash any material that is not pre-shrunk before making up. In the case of fitted covers it is best to replace the cushion pad when the fabric is still slightly damp. This allows the fabric to stretch back into shape as it dries. As with curtains, always dry clean lined items as there is no guarantee that both fabrics will shrink equally when washed. This also applies to items that are trimmed with rope, fringes, and tassels.

Keep any leftover fabric when you have finished a soft furnishings project. You can use fabric scraps to test out cleaning processes before you tackle the item itself and to repair damages or stains. Leftovers will also help you colormatch any new fabrics and furnishings you may want to add to your room.

PREPARATION FOR PAINTING

Preparation of surfaces in a room is vitally important – and the most laborious part of the job. The more time you spend rubbing walls down with sandpaper, filling cracks and holes with filler, and so on, the better the finished results will be.

If there is any old wallpaper on the wall, strip it off and start from scratch. You can hire powerful electric strippers for the job which will be hard work but efficient. Acrylic solvents for wallpaper are available but take longer and are less satisfying to use.

If walls are crumbling or cracked have them re-plastered. The longer you then leave the new plaster to dry before redecorating the better. In a centrally heated house in a reasonable climate a month should be enough. Decorate with water-based paint so the plaster can breathe and continue to dry out thoroughly. Even so, a loadbearing wall may still produce hairline cracks as much as four months later. You can carefully fill and repaint these in a room painted with latex (emulsion), but it is impossible to repair cracks effectively if glazes and paint effects have been used.

Cleaning Brushes

Good brushes are not cheap, but if given tender loving care they will last and give excellent service. Acrylic glazes and paints dry quickly, so clean your brushes as soon as possible after use. Dunk the brush into warm water and liquid detergent when you have finished painting. Then take a wire brush and brush firmly through the bristles to remove any paint that remains. If brushes are left dirty and the paint dries hard, soften them with denatured alcohol (methylated spirits) before washing in warm water and mild detergent. Soft-haired brushes need particular care and should never be left to dry without washing. If you use oil-based paint, clean brushes with mineral spirits (white spirit) followed by warm water and mild detergent.

GLOSSARY — SOFT FURNISHINGS

Appliqué: the application of a second layer of fabric onto a base cloth to create a pattern.

Architrave brackets: slim brackets, usually made of brass, fitted to the wall or window frame and used to support a pole for a blind or curtain.

Basting: a long stitch, used to hold two or more layers of fabric together temporarily.

Batting: a fluffy, fibrous material used in quilts and to stuff and shape goblet pleats.

Blackout lining: a special lining that blocks out all light. It is made of a layer of opaque material between two layers of cotton fabric.

Bolster: a simple, sausage-shaped cushion.

Box cushion: a cushion covered with a top and a bottom section cut to the shape of the seat, plus a boxing strip to cover the sides of the cushion.

Box pleats: a heading of flat pleats at the front of a curtain.

Brocade: a heavy fabric woven to create raised patterns and including some gold or silver thread. Brocade was traditionally made in silk, but modern versions are also available in cotton.

Buckram: a stiffened fabric used to give shape to pleated headings and tiebacks. It is made of cotton or jute and available in several different weights. Normal buckram must be sewn in, but fusible buckram can be sealed to the fabric by the heat of an iron.

Burlap (hessian): an open-weave, rough-textured fabric made of fiber from the jute plant. It can be used for blinds, cushions, and table covers for a natural look.

Café clip: decorative clip that grips the top of a curtain or blind and encircles a pole support.

Calico: a raw, unbleached cotton fabric with a plain weave. Originally used as a lining and backing fabric, it is now popular for making simple curtains and blinds.

Canvas: a strong, tightly woven cotton with an even texture. Canvas is useful wherever strength is a priority, such as for directors' chairs and outdoor furniture.

Chenille: a soft fabric made from fluffy cotton yarn, which gives it its soft texture. The name comes from the French for hairy caterpillar.

Chiffon: a light, translucent fabric made of silk or nylon.

Chintz: a fabric usually made from cotton and generally printed with floral patterns on a cream or light ground.

Cording: a system of cords threaded through rings fitted to the back of a blind so that it can be raised and lowered .

Corduroy: a hardwearing, ribbed fabric that is soft to the touch. It is suitable for fitted cushions and slipcovers.

Crewel-work: an embroidered surface pattern, often painstakingly hand-stitched in rich, floral designs. It is very effective used on bedspreads and cushions.

Damask: a woven fabric with a special weave that produces a raised pattern and flat background. Damask is made in different fibers, such as wool, silk, and cotton, and is suitable for curtains, cushions, and slipcovers. It is also traditionally used for table linen.

Dormer window: a small window that is set into and often projects from the slope of a roof.

Dowel rod: a slender wooden rod that is inserted into fabric pockets at the back of a blind, such as a Roman blind, enabling it to be pulled up in neat folds.

Drop weight: a holder made of brass or wood into which the cords of a blind are threaded.

Dupion: a lightweight silk fabric with a textured surface, suitable for curtains and for scatter cushions. Artificial dupion, made of viscose and acetate, is also available.

Finial: decorative end pieces fitted to a curtain pole to provide a visual finishing touch and to keep the rings on the pole.

French pleats: also known as pencil pleats, this heading is made up of groups of three slim pleats spaced across the curtain. The pleats can be made with special heading tape but look even better if hand-sewn.

Gingham: a simple, checked fabric made of cotton.

Goblet pleats: a hand-sewn heading made of rounded pleats stuffed with batting (wadding) so they keep their shape.

Grommet (eyelet): a two-part metal ring used as a heading for curtains or blinds. A punch and dye set punches a hole in the fabric and fits the two parts of the grommet (eyelet), one on each side of the fabric.

Grosgrain (petersham): a silk textile with a ribbed surface, often used for making ribbon.

Heading: the finish at the top of a curtain or blind. Styles range from simple gathered headings made with tape to more complex pleated headings.

Herringbone: fabric with a diagonally patterned weave, which gives it a chunky texture. It is strong and hardwearing so a good choice for curtains.

Interlining: a combed cotton fabric placed between the main fabric of a curtain or blind and the lining to provide insulation as well as body and weight.

Lath: a piece of timber, usually 2 x 1in (5 x 2.5cm), to which the top of a blind is fitted. The lath is then attached to the wall, ceiling, or window frame.

Lath and fascia: a structure fitted in front of a curtain rod to conceal it. The lath is fitted at right angles to the wall and the fascia fitted to the front of it. The rod is fitted to the underside of the lath and is concealed by the fascia. The lath and fascia are generally covered in the same fabric as the curtains.

Linen: a beautiful, hardwearing fabric made from flax. Linen may be finely woven or have a more open texture. A range of colored and printed versions is available but linen generally looks its best in natural shades.

Lining: a cotton fabric used to back curtains and blinds. Standard lining is made of a tightly woven cotton fabric called sateen, which keeps its shape well. It is generally used in cream or white, but a range of colored linings is also available.

Mitering: a technique used to make a neat, flat corner where the side hem and base hem of a curtain or blind meet.

Moleskin: a hardwearing cotton fabric with a soft velvety pile. Ideal for cushions and slipcovers when durability is important.

Muslin: a fine, translucent cotton. Most muslin is plain but some have a white printed design to add texture. Muslin can be hung behind curtains to provide daytime privacy.

Organza: a lightweight, translucent fabric with a slightly stiff texture.

Pelmet: a panel, made of wood or fabric stiffener and covered with fabric, that hides the top of a curtain. The pelmet is fixed to a wooden support fixed above the curtain rod.

Pencil pleats: *see* French pleats.

Piping: a neat, practical finish for the edges of curtains and blinds made from strips of fabric cut on the bias (diagonally across the fabric) and stitched around lengths of cord.

Poplin: a light, cotton fabric with a corded surface made by using thicker weft threads than warp threads.

Quilt: a padded bedcover with batting (wadding) sandwiched between two layers of fabric. All layers are stitched through to hold them together.

Recess window: a window that is set back into the wall, so that you can hang a curtain or blind inside the recess instead of on the wall.

Return: the part of a curtain or blind that goes round the end of a rod or lath.

Rod pocket (slot) heading: a sleeve of fabric at the top of a curtain or blind into which you slide a pole as a support.

Self-pelmet: fabric at the top of a curtain which is folded and stitched to look like a separate section.

Selvedge: the tightly woven edges of a width of fabric.

Squab cushion: a cushion that is tailor-made to fit the shape of a chair and frequently secured to the struts with fabric ties.

Swag: an elaborate, decorative drape, placed at the top of a window to hang in front of the curtain headings.

Taffeta: a crisp, finely woven silk fabric. It has warp and weft threads of subtly different colors which give it an everchanging surface. It drapes well and is suitable for full-length curtains.

Tapestry: a heavy, machine-woven fabric that imitates the look of traditional hand-woven tapestries. Its rich texture makes it ideal for heavy curtains and blinds.

Thermal lining: a cotton lining fabric that is coated with a layer of aluminum on one side for insulation.

Tieback: a device made of fabric, rope, ribbon, or other material used to tie a curtain back.

Toile de Jouy: a cotton fabric originally made in the French town of Jouy and printed with scenes of country life.

Twill: a sturdy, hardwearing fabric, woven to produce parallel diagonal lines.

Velvet: a woven fabric with a short, thick pile on one side. The pile absorbs or reflects light, depending on how the light falls, making the fabric appear darker or lighter. Therefore, velvet must always be cut so that the pile runs in the same direction on all pieces.

Voile: a white, semi-transparent fabric made of silk or cotton.

Wadding: a fluffy, fibrous material used in quilts and to stuff goblet pleats.

Warp threads: the threads of a fabric that travel up and down.

Weft threads: the threads of a fabric that travel from side to side.

Weights: round metal discs that are placed in the hems of curtains to help them hang better.

GLOSSARY — PAINT AND PAPER

Architrave: the molding that surrounds a door or window.

Aging: a technique for simulating the effects of time and wear on a freshly painted surface. Also called antiquing.

Baseboard: a narrow board that runs around the base of walls.

Basecoat: the first coat of paint for most decorative paint finishes, applied before the glaze.

Beeswax: wax produced by bees. Used by decorators to protect and shine a painted finish.

Border: a design around the edge of a panel, wall, or floor, which may be stenciled, printed, or painted freehand.

Bronze powder: a metallic powder available in several shades. This can be used to mix metallic paint and is an excellent substitute for gold leaf.

Calcimine (distemper): a paint with a chalky flat finish, made of a mixture of pigment, whiting, and glue size.

Chair rail: a molding that runs round the wall at the approximate height of the back of an upright chair.

Colorwashing: a simple but effective paint effect with a translucent finish. Acrylic glaze is applied over a light basecoat and brushed out with large, sweeping brush strokes or wiped gently with a soft cloth.

Combing: a simple paint effect in which a special tool is used to comb through the top color of glaze to reveal the base color beneath. Further layers can be added to make check effects.

Crackleglaze: a finish produced by using two varnishes that work against each other to produce a crazed effect.

Crown molding (cornice): a molding that runs round the ceiling at the top of a wall.

Decoupage: the technique of covering a surface with a collection of cutout paper images. The images are carefully cut out, stuck down, and varnished.

Denatured alcohol (methylated spirits): an alcohol-based solvent used for cleaning brushes and other processes.

Distemper: *see* calcimine.

Distressing: a technique for making a surface such as a door or baseboard look naturally aged. The surface is painted with eggshell and then glazed. The glaze is then gently lifted with steel wool.

Dragging: a traditional painted effect achieved by dragging a glazed wall with a fine-bristled dragging brush to create an even, linear look. The dragged finish can also be flogged – hit with a special brush called a flogger – to break up the stripes.

Faux finishes: finishes that imitate another material such as wood, tortoiseshell, or marble.

Flock: a wallpaper with a raised velvety pattern.

Frieze: the area of a wall between the crown molding (cornice) and picture rail. Also a band of decoration, usually just below the crown molding (cornice), that may be wallpapered, stenciled, or painted freehand.

Flogger: long hogshair brush used to make a coarser finish when dragging, and in woodgraining.

Floor paint: a range of specially tough paint suitable for use on wood, linoleum, and concrete.

Fresco: a method of watercolor painting, usually on a wall or ceiling, executed before the plaster is dry.

Frottage: the process of gently pressing newspaper onto wet paint and removing it quickly to reveal an uneven, organic finish.

Gilding: a specialty technique for applying gold to surfaces such as furniture or picture frames.

Glaze: a translucent mixture of glaze and pigment colors used for paint effects. Oil-based and water-based glazes are available.

Gloss: oil-based paint with a high-sheen, glossy finish.

Gold leaf: sheets of gold beaten to a wafer thinness and used in gilding.

Grouting: a fine plaster for filling the spaces between tiles or stone blocks. On trompe l'oeil blocks, grouting can be imitated with painted lines applied with an artist's brush.

Lacquering: a technique for simulating the high-gloss finish of Chinese and Japanese lacquer.

Latex (emulsion): a flat, water-based paint suitable for use on walls and ceilings.

Latex eggshell: water-based paint with a silky sheen. Eggshell is suitable for woodwork and as a base for acrylic glaze on woodwork.

Limewash: a mixture of lime and water, which can be used as a decorative, protective paint.

Liming: A technique which imitates the old custom of painting wooden furniture with diluted limewash left over from painting the walls. Instead, liming wax (a mixture of beeswax and whiting) is worked into the wood. The surface is then polished, leaving a residue of white wax in the grain.

Lining paper: plain, flat wallpaper used to line the walls of a room to disguise poor quality plasterwork. Lining paper should be sealed with diluted undercoat before painting.

Marbling: the process of imitating marble. An acrylic glaze is applied over a light base and softened with ragging and a soft brush to achieve marble-like markings.

Masking: a technique used to create a straight painted or stippled line. The masking tape is applied either side of the intended line. The paint is applied between the tape and the tape is removed.

Molding: ornamental and continuous lines of grooving or projections. Chair rails, architraves, pictures rails, crown moldings (cornices), and baseboards are usually molded.

Oil eggshell: an oil-based, durable paint with a satin finish, ideal for woodwork.

Paint kettle: a small, bucketlike container, made of metal or plastic, in which small quantities of paint can be carried easily.

Picture rail: horizontal molding originally designed for hanging pictures. In an average-sized room, it is usually about 17in (43cm) from the crown molding (cornice). The gap between the two increases in a taller room.

Pigment: coloring matter used in paints.

Plumbline: a weighted string used for marking verticals.

Primary colors: the colors from which all others can be mixed. The primary colors are red, yellow, and blue. They combine to form secondary colors.

Rag rolling: a technique in which glaze is applied and then rolled with a sausage shape of cotton rag which removes glaze irregularly. Several layers of glaze can be rolled.

Ragging: a technique in which glaze is applied over a basecoat and gently dabbed off with a bunched cotton rag. This reveals the underlying color and creates a delicate subtle effect.

Sandpaper: abrasive paper available in varying degrees of coarseness, used for rubbing down paintwork.

Secondary colors: colors made by mixing two primary colors. Secondary colors mixed together make tertiary colors.

Shellac: a resinous varnish.

Spirit level: a glass tube partly filled with spirit; the position of the air bubble in the spirit indicates whether the surface is level.

Sponging: colored glaze is applied over a basecoat and lifted off while still wet with a damp sponge. Alternatively, successive layers of glaze can be added to the basecoat using a sponge.

Steel wool: an abrasive pad made from fine shavings of steel, used in techniques such as distressing. Steel wool is available in varying degrees of coarseness.

Stenciling: the technique of producing images or patterns with stencils. The intended design is traced onto the paperboard (card) and cut out with a craft knife. The stencil is then securely held onto the wall and various colors are punched through the cutout holes with a suitable stenciling or stippling brush.

Stippling: an effect applied to glaze for broken color work. Boxlike square bristle brushes are used to achieve this effect. Once the wet glaze is applied to the wall, it is vigorously and systematically punched with the stippling brush, creating millions of tiny dots.

Tongue-and-groove: two boards that are slotted into each other. The protecting tongue of one is slotted into the groove of the other. Tongue-and-groove boarding can be used to cover walls.

Tortoiseshell: a faux finish that imitates the shell of a tortoise. The area is prepared and glazed and daubs of darker, more concentrated glaze are added. These are softened with a brush to create a mottled effect.

Trompe l'oeil: the art of deceiving the eye by making a flat painted area look like a three-dimensional image with painted shadow lines.

Turpentine: a resinous solvent mixed into some paints and varnishes.

Varnish: a protective resinous solution produced in three levels of sheen – flat, satin, and gloss. Two main types are available. Water-based acrylic varnish does not yellow with age and is elastic so does not easily crack. Oil-based varnish is slower-drying and tends to yellow, bringing extra warmth and depth to colors.

Wet-and-dry sandpaper: abrasive used with water to achieve a really smooth finish.

Whiting: finely ground calcium carbonate used in liming wax.

Woodgraining: the technique of making a cheap wooden door, or other wooden surface, look as if it is made of mahogany, oak, or other expensive wood. The surface is glazed and appropriate grain markings are added with woodgraining brushes.

INDEX

Page numbers in *italic* refer to illustrations.

ACKNOWLEDGMENTS

I would like to thank the team of talented people who created this book. First and foremost are Anne Boston and Jane Hughes, who wrote the text, interpreting and developing my ideas for the book brilliantly. Anne's sections, "Decorating with Style" and "Decorating Solutions", are models of well-informed writing delivered with a lightness of touch; Jane's sections, "Decorating with Soft Furnishings" and "Decorating with Paint and Paper", are written with flair and with real insight into the practicalities of home decorating.

Chris Wood designed a lovely, fresh look for the book, one which is both elegant and flexible. Layout artists Ruth Prentice and Alison Shackleton put her designs into action beautifully. Sorcha Hitchcox instinctively and accurately translated a picture research brief into exciting transparencies.

Claire Waite edited and managed all the strands of a complex project on a tight schedule with great skill, astonishing calm, and apparent ease. She was aided by Alison Wormleighton's meticulous proofreading.

I would also like to thank Susan Berry, the editor who made my involvement with this project possible, and Oliver Kassman, my son, who for weeks gamely tolerated a mother obsessed with pictures of the insides of houses.

Picture credits

With the exception of those listed below, all photographs in this book are the copyright of Kiln House Books. The publisher and author would like to thank the following sources for their kind permission to reproduce the photographs listed.

Elizabeth Whiting Associates page 144

Robert Harding Syndication

Page 1 and 180 Simon Upton/Homes and Gardens; page 9 Tim Beddow/Homes and Interiors; page 14 Steve Dalton/Woman and Home; page 15 Tom Leighton/Homes and Gardens; page 18 Tom Leighton/Homes and Gardens; page 24 Dominic Blackmore/Homes and Ideas; page 32 James Merrell/Homes and Gardens;

page 36 James Merrell/Homes and Gardens; page 38 and jacket Christopher Drake/Homes and Gardens; page 41 Tom Leighton/Options; page 46 Andrew Cameron/Country Homes and Interiors; page 52 Lucinda Symons/Country Homes and Interiors; page 62 Gavin Kingcome/Homes and Gardens; page 64 center Christopher Drake/Country Homes and Interiors; page 74 Fritz von der Schulenberg/Country Homes and Interiors; page 82 Joshua Pulman/Country Homes and Interiors; page 88 Christopher Drake/Homes and Gardens; page 100 Mark Luscombe-Whyte/Country Homes and Interiors; page 104 Brian Harrison/Country Homes and Interiors; page 108 Ideal Home; page 112 Andreas von Einsiedel/Homes and Gardens; page 116 Tom Leighton/Homes and Gardens; page 122 and jacket Lucinda Symons/Ideal Home; page 134 top right James Merrell/Homes and Gardens; page 142 Bill Reavell/Homes and Ideas; page 182 Christopher Drake/Homes and Gardens; page 226 David Giles/Homes and Ideas; page 236 Hugh Palmer/Country Homes and Interiors; page 249 Tim Beddow/Homes and Gardens; page 256 Michael James; page 258 James Merrell/Country Homes and Interiors; page 266 Tim Imrie/Country Homes and Interiors; page 272 and jacket Dominic Blackmore/Homes and Ideas; page 278 Christopher Drake/Woman's Journal; page 282 Jonathan Pilkington/Homes and Gardens; page 290 Homes and Gardens; page 292 Polly Wreford/ Country Homes and Interiors; page 314 and jacket Tim Rose/Ideal Home; page 330 Mark Fiennes/Homes and Gardens; page 332 Joanne Cowie/Country Homes and Interiors; page 334 Mark Bolton/Homes and Gardens; page 336 Christopher Drake/Country Homes and Interiors; page 338 Ideal Home; page 340 Ken Kirkwood/Homes and Gardens; page 344 Mark Luscombe-Whyte/Homes and Gardens; page 347 Simon Brown/Country Homes and Interiors; page 354 Fritz von der Schulenburg/Country Homes and Interiors; page 364 Ideal Home; page 374 Ed Davies/Ideal Home; page 380 Fritz von der Schulenburg/Country Homes and Interiors; page 387 Homes and Gardens; page 390 Mark Luscombe-Whyte/Homes and Gardens; page 400 Polly Wreford/Country Homes and Interiors; page 402 Dominic Blackmore/Homes and Ideas; page 405 Dominic Blackmore/Homes and Ideas; page 410 Dominic Blackmore/Homes and Ideas; page 414 Simon Upton/Options; page 420 Tom Leighton/Homes and Gardens.